and Roses

Favorite Recipes from Twelve Years of Catering – and More!

Debby Nothaft

1st WORLD LIBRARY
Literary Society

• Austin • Fairfield • Delhi

Xmas 2016

Andi & Hanna,
I know this is not strictly VEGAN, BUT the author is a mom of a colleague, I know you two will enjoy the veggie essence!!
xoxo
Br.

Cabbages and Roses

Debby Nothaft

° 1st World Library – Literary Society, 2003
809 South 2nd Street
Fairfield, IA 52556
www.1stworldlibrary.org
First Edition

LCCN: 2003116311

ISBN: 1-595409-99-8

All rights reserved. No part of this book may be reproduced or utilized in any form or by any means, electronic or mechanical, including photocopying or recording, or by any information storage and retrieval system, without permission in writing from the publisher.

Readers interested in obtaining information
on 1stWorld Library: • Publishing Services
• Contributions •Book Conversion
• Convert-On-Demand / Print-On-Demand contact
www.1stworldlibrary.org

Dedication

To my dear children, Marsten, David and Rowie, who are always in my heart,
and bright.
From stormy weather to clear skies
we fly together.
And from his perch on the other side,
Marsten brings us blue skies,
and wide.

Acknowledgements

Thank-you, the "dear hearts and gentle people" of my spiritual family for letting me
serve you, for helping me find my wings and my Home, for being my friend.

Thanks to son, David, for the enthusiasm and devotion to get his mom moving on
this new endeavor, pushing me along (no mean feat!), until I, too, took fire.

Thanks to Christopher Cook for the original "firing-up" of this project; to Keith
Cobb, Beth Kennett and Kirk Neff for their help.
And thanks to Claudette Sandoval for her help as the computer whiz she is and the
fun hanging out with her.

Table of Contentment

Cabbages and Roses

The Far Reach

The poet Robert Browning gave us a dear truth when he wrote: "A man's reach must exceed his grasp, or what's a heaven for!?" Too true! We don't want to sink in the mud! And we need our dreams as seeds to grow.

And yet there is the finest divinity even in the simplest of things: a kitten playing in a shaft of sunlight- true exquisiteness!

A simple unpretentious food dish, prepared with care and attention, is purely divine and sustaining. Add a dash of gourmet, and we have succeeded to reach for the stars as we ever expand out in our personal self-expression.

Recipes are always evolving. They are an art form, like snowflakes, or dance steps. The food served takes into accounts the time, place, season, weather, mood of the cook, the occasion and the people eating. These things are not chiseled in stone.

When I was a little girl, I used to get mad at my Dad because he never followed a recipe the way it was given. Now, I see my own daughter taking great delight in following to perfection the instructions given (unless, of course, I'm the one giving them to her) Now, I do the same as my Dad, and in understanding is forgiveness. Sometimes I like the recipe as is. And other times I use it as a springboard of inspiration to new and different heights! Have fun!

Even after moving to New Mexico in 1992 I couldn't keep my nose out of cookbooks and ovens, and more adventures. So more delicious dishes have been collected along the way, their essences sprinkled here and there in this bookish endeavor. -one hundred new recipes for this new edition.

Savories, Sauces and Tidbits

Spatulas and Roses

A very important tool of the trade is a sawed-off rubber spatula. I came across this find in the usual mindless ferment of fervent activity. To prevent scorching on the bottom of a particular pot of sauce, I used what came to reach easily- a rubber spatula! Lo and behold, it did melt a bit. To save the day, my neck, and the rubber spatula, we cut off the wimped out part, finding the rest made of sterner stuff and still able to get those sticky pot corners. We finished the day, and many more, smelling like roses, thanks to this handy hearty tool!

Sinfully Seasoned French Bread
About 15 slices

1	loaf French or Italian bread, unsliced
4-6	cloves garlic, peeled
½	c. extra virgin olive oil
¼	c. butter
1½	c. whipping cream
½	c. grated Romano cheese
½	c. Parmesan cheese
2	Tbs. butter
♥	minced parsley
♥	fresh ground pepper

Cut bread diagonally into 1" slices. In food processor or blender, chop garlic and add olive oil gradually to make a thin paste. In saucepan melt butter and add oil and garlic.

Using brush or rubber spatula slather mixture on crust and inside of bread. Bake at 350° for 15 minutes, or until top is crispy. Now, you might want to stop right at this point and serve bread as is. You certainly won't loose out. If you want to add even more decadent richness, well read on!

While bread is in the oven, heat cream in heavy saucepan. Do not boil. Slowly whisk in cheeses to smoothness. Add butter; keep warm. Just before serving place bread in warmed platter with sides and pour sauce over all. Garnish with pepper and parsley and serve!

Bleu Cheese Fillo Fingers
3 dozen pieces

6   sheets fillo, thawed but well covered
½   c. or more butter, melted
4   oz. cream cheese, soft
4   oz. crumbled bleu cheese
1   Tbs. cream

Cream together cheeses and cream.

Butter one sheet fillo. Top with second and butter. Using 1/3 of cheese, roll a thick log of it positioned along one lengthwise edge of buttered fillo.

Roll the fillo up like a log with the cheese inside. Place on un-greased cookie sheet. Butter all. Repeat 2 more times, making 3 logs.

Bake at 375° for 10-12 minutes till brown and bubbly. Slice in 1 inch pieces and serve hot.

I haven't met a fillo log yet that doesn't spill some of its innards while baking. But never fear- the crisp cheese is one of the best parts!

Cheddar Cheese Puffs
2-3 dozen tidbits

¼   c. milk
¼   c. water
¼   c. butter
♥   pinches salt, pepper, nutmeg
½   c. flour
2   eggs
2   c. grated sharp cheddar cheese

Heat milk, water, butter and seasonings to boiling in saucepan. Plop in flour all at once and stir vigorously with a wooden spoon till it forms a solid mass that comes away from the sides of the pan.

Remove from heat and, while hot, beat in eggs and cheese till paste is shiny and smooth.

Drop by teaspoonfuls on greased cookie sheet about 1" apart and bake at 400° (no less!) for 15 minutes, then at 350° for about 10 minutes until golden and puffed. Serve warm.

Cheese squares
3 dozen

1   loaf unsliced bread, crust
     removed, cut in 1½"
     squares
½   c. butter
1½ c. grated cheddar cheese
3   oz. cream cheese
2   egg whites

Melt butter and cheeses together over low heat, blending well. Cool partially. Whip egg whites stiff, but not dry. Carefully but thoroughly fold in cheese mixture. Dip bread squares in cheese, covering all sides, and place on cookie sheet. Cover and refrigerate overnight. Bake at 375°, 15 minutes. Serve hot.

Crab Rangoon
30 tidbits

½   pkg. fresh wonton squares,
     3"x3" (freeze rest, to be
     used another time)
1   6 oz. can crab pieces,
     drained
8   oz. soft cream cheese
2   green onions, minced

Whip cream cheese till fluffy and fold in rest. Place a teaspoonful on a single wonton wrapper. Wet 2 adjoining sides with a finger dipped in water and run along the edges. Fold to carefully line up and meet the opposite corners, creating a triangle. Press firmly to seal. Fold in the 2 outside points, or leave as is. Store under plastic.

Heat 1" oil to medium hot, so one side of wonton browns in a few minutes. Turn and brown other side. Fry only 5-6 at time. Overheating causes filling to leak thru.
Pineapple Plum Sweet-Sour Sauce makes a good dipping sauce.

Honey Baked Wings
15-20 pieces

3   lbs. chicken wings,
     tips cut off and split
½   c. honey
¼   c. soy sauce
¼   c. brown sugar
¼   c. ketchup
½   tsp. garlic powder
½   tsp. onion powder
♥   dashes hot sauce

Place wings in a non-metal shallow baking dish and sprinkle with salt, pepper and paprika.

Combine ingredients and spread ½ over wings. Bake 30 minutes, at 375°, basting twice. Turn and spread on rest of sauce. Bake 30 minutes, basting more.

Fillo Turnovers-Curried Chicken or Turkey
40 bite-size pieces

1 pound fillo dough, thawed according to directions on package

3-4 cubes (3/4 -1 lb.), butter, melted and hot

Filling:

3 c. minced cooked chicken or turkey

2 Tbs. butter

2 Tbs. flour

2 tsp. curry powder

$\frac{1}{2}$ tsp. turmeric

$\frac{1}{2}$ tsp. black mustard seed

$\frac{1}{2}$ tsp. salt

$\frac{1}{2}$ tsp. tarragon

♥ pinch cayenne or pepper

1 c. milk

$\frac{1}{2}$ c. fine chopped toasted almonds, pecans, or walnuts

$\frac{1}{4}$ c. currants or raisins

♥ grated rind of 1 orange

To make filling: Melt butter; stir in flour and seasonings and cook over low heat a few minutes. Add milk and, using whisk, stir and cook till thickened, about 5 minutes.
stir in nuts, raisins, orange peel and chicken. Cool completely.

To assemble: Using a wide pastry brush (3" is good), butter a cookie sheet and set it to one side of your working area. On a flat surface place 1 sheet of fillo and brush lightly and evenly with butter. Lay another sheet on top and butter it. Cut into 6 equal strips, widthwise.

Place 1 Tbs. filling at a bottom corner of one strip and fold that corner up and over to the top edge of the strip- thus making a triangle. Continue folding the triangle to the end as you would a flag (up, over, down, over, etc.) Easy after a couple!

Place on cookie sheet and butter top and sides. Continue with all strips. Butter and cut 2 more sheets, and continue, using up filling.

Bake at 425° for 15 minutes, until golden brown. Serve hot.

Variation: Substitute $\frac{1}{2}$ the Spinach Turnover recipe for the chicken. Or try a nice cheese filling - or curried potatoes, or, or.......

Filled Little Chicken Puffs
4 dozen little ones

These are an elegant substitute for fussy fillo, using the same chicken filling, or any other you like.

1   recipe Curry Chicken Turnover filling

Puffs
- ½ c. milk
- ½ c. water
- ¼ c. butter
- ¼ c. salt
- ἐ pinch nutmeg
- ἐ pinch pepper
- 1 c. flour
- 4 eggs
- 1 c. grated Swiss cheese

Heat milk, butter, seasoning in saucepan, medium high heat till it boils. Add flour all at once and beat to a smooth paste. Add eggs one at a time, beating until smooth and shiny. Mix in cheese.

Drop by round teaspoonfuls on greased sheet 1" apart. Bake 400° until golden, 20-25 minutes. Cool completely. Cut off tops, pull out any moist innards and fill with chicken, and put tops back on. Bake at 375° till heated thru, about 5-8 minutes. You can wait an hour before baking before they get soggy.

Savory Chicken Liver Tidbits
4-6 servings

- 1 lb. chicken livers, cut in bite size pieces
- ¼ c. butter
- ¼ c. olive oil
- 1 clove garlic, minced
- 1 tsp. oregano
- ¼ c. fresh lemon juice
- ἐ salt, pepper, to taste

Heat butter, oil and garlic and oregano. Saute liver 5 minutes. Stir in lemon juice and seasoning. Cook a few more minutes, but don't overcook.

Serve with crackers or French bread to soak up the yummy juices. (It's my Jewish blood!)

Rolled Grapes
About 50 grapes

- 4 oz. soft cream cheese
- 2-3 Tbs. milk
- 1½ c. toasted pecans, finely chopped

Beat cream cheese and milk together to make a smooth paste that will adhere thickly to a grape rolled in it. Coat grape with cream cheese and then roll in nuts. Chill before serving.

Spicy Sweet Potato Fritters
30 small

1   lb. sweet potato, (1 medium) peeled, grated
1   Tbs. grated fine, peeled ginger
2   Tbs. fresh lemon juice
1   Tbs. sugar
½   tsp. hot pepper flakes
½   tsp. salt
2   Tbs. flour
2   eggs

☺   vegetable oil for frying

Mix everything together well.

In heavy pan heat 1 inch oil over moderate high heat, to 360° on a deep fat thermometer. Drop by tablespoonful into hot oil; flatten the middles a bit with the spoon. Fry for 2 minutes, or until golden. Turn to fry other side. Drain on paper towels.
Try serving with Mango Sauce.

Mushroom and Leek Strudel with Artichoke Hearts
24 pieces

4   Tbs. butter
1   tsp. Spike seasoning salt
1   lb. mushrooms
2   tsp. fresh lemon juice
1   clove garlic, minced
2   Tbs. flour
1   large leek, sliced thin, with top green part
½   c. half & half
¼   tsp. salt
¼   tsp. pepper
1   small jar marinated artichoke hearts, chopped
½   lb. fillo dough, 10 sheets
½   c. butter, melted and hot
¼   c. bread crumbs

Melt butter and stir in Spike, cooking a few moments. Stir in mushrooms, garlic and lemon juice. Cook 5-10 minutes, stirring often, until liquid is absorbed.

Blend in flour and cook 5 minutes more, stirring.

Add leek, reduce heat and add cream, salt and pepper. Simmer until thick, stirring often. Stir in artichoke hearts. Cool.

Place fillo sheet on towel. Brush with butter and sprinkle with 1 tsp. breadcrumbs. Repeat 4 times.

Mound ½ of mixture along one long edge of fillo, making a strip 1½" wide. Lifting towel, roll the fillo up lightly, tucking in sides.
Place seam side down on buttered baking sheet. Repeat with second strudel. Bake at 375° for 25 minutes, until golden. Cut and serve warm.

Southwestern Dip
Party size
My little buddy Rhonda served this to us when first we arrived in New Mexico. It is a fun party food. Her fancy Morgan show horse is fun too!

1	28 oz. can refried beans, pinto or black beans
2	c. prepared salsa
1½	c. sour cream
1	1¼ oz. package taco seasoning
4	ripe avocados
2	Tbs. lemon or lime juice
1	tsp. salt
½	tsp. garlic sauce
2-3	c. grated cheddar and/or Jack cheese
2	c. chopped tomatoes
2	c. minced onion, or 2 c. sliced green onion
1	16 oz. can olives, sliced

On a 16" serving platter, spread beans in a level, round layer. Spread salsa evenly over beans. Mix sour cream and taco seasoning together and spread over salsa.

Mash peeled and pitted avocados with lemon juice, salt and garlic powder and spread over sour cream.

Sprinkle with cheese, tomato, onions and olives.

Serve with tortilla chips. (For less fat, cut flour tortillas in sixths and bake on cookie sheet 350° 5 minutes each side, or until crispy-brown.)

Candied Walnuts
3 cups
These are a tasty snack, good for a party, or add to salads and vegetables. Present them prettily packaged as a gift

3	cups raw walnuts
½	c. sugar
¼	c. water

Drop walnuts into a quart of boiling water and boil 5 minutes. Drain in a sieve and rinse briefly.

Add the sugar and water to the saucepan. Bring to a boil and add walnuts. Stir the nuts until all the liquid disappears.

Spread the nuts on a cookie sheet lined with parchment or tin foil. Bake at 350° 7-8 minutes on one side. Turn nuts and bake 7-8 minutes on other. Will get a toastie flavor. Sprinkle with salt while just out of the oven.

Try substituting pecans or cashews. Almonds take longer to bake crisp.

Tahini Dip
1¼ cups

3 Tbs. vegetable oil
3 Tbs. fresh lemon juice
3 Tbs. tahini
1 Tbs. tamari
1 tsp. rice or white vinegar
¼ c. chopped onion
4" celery stalk
3" carrot piece

1 clove garlic, cut in pieces
¼ tsp. pepper

Blend all together in blender till smooth and thick. If too thick, thin with a little water.

Cuke Canapes
40 pieces

2 medium cucumbers

Combine in small bowl:
4 oz. soft cream cheese
2 Tbs. minced parsley
2 Tbs. minced chives, or
  ½ tsp. onion powder, or
  both
1 Tbs. mayonnaise or
  plain yogurt
1 tsp. fresh lemon juice
½ tsp. horseradish
🌶 stuffed green olive slices

Cut ends off cukes; place on end and draw fork tines or tip of potato peeler lengthwise down cucumber to score peel all the way around. Cut into ½" slices and line up on paper towel.

Spread or pipe each slice with cheese dollop or flower. Garnish with green olive slices and sprinkle lightly with paprika and pepper.

Artichoke Dip
2 cups

1 12 oz. can artichoke hearts, unseasoned
2/3 c. mayonnaise
½ c. sour cream
½ c. Parmesan
🌶 salt, pepper

Drain the artichoke hearts,

squeezing them dry, and chop fine. Mix with rest of ingredients and pour into small, nice-for-serving baking dish, and bake 20 minutes at 350° till good and hot.

Serve with crackers or crunchy vegetables, especially celery.

Hot Crab Dip
2 cups

1	6 oz. can crab meat
$\frac{1}{4}$	c. mayonnaise
8	oz. cream cheese, soft
1	Tbs. minced parsley
1	Tbs. minced chives
1	Tbs. fresh lemon juice
$\frac{1}{2}$	tsp. onion powder
$\frac{1}{2}$	tsp. prepared horseradish
🌶	salt and pepper

Break up crab and mix with mayonnaise. Whip cream cheese with milk and add to crab with seasonings. Salt and pepper, to taste. Fill baking dish and heat in oven at 350° until bubbly and brown on edges, 20 minutes, or so. Serve with crackers or celery sticks as an appetizer. Or use as a sauce over pasta or veggies.

Hot Mexican Cheese Dip
2 cups

4	oz. soft cream cheese
2	c. sharp cheddar cheese, grated
1	4 oz. can chopped green chilies
2	Tbs. minced jalapenos, canned or fresh
$\frac{1}{4}$	c. minced or grated onion
$\frac{1}{2}$	tsp. garlic powder

Whip all together well. Place in greased baking dish and heat till bubbly, at 350°, about 20- 25 minutes. Serve with chips, crackers, veggies, etc.

Use rubber gloves if you prepare fresh jalapeno. On your skin pepper will burn for hours. Do I speak from experience? Of course!

Guacamole
1 avocado for 2-3 people

Mash ripe avocado with your choice of the following:
- 🌶 salsa from the jar
- 🌶 mayonnaise
- 🌶 minced green onion
- 🌶 minced cilantro
- 🌶 fresh chopped tomato
- 🌶 garlic powder
- 🌶 onion powder
- 🌶 Tabasco
- 🌶 salt, pepper
- 🌶 lime or lemon juice

May I suggest 1 tsp. vinegar per avocado. Something about vinegar that brings out the best of both worlds.

Chive Dip
2 cups

Blend together:
1½ c. sour cream
½ c. yogurt
½ c. minced chives
½ tsp. pepper
½ tsp. salt

♥ several dashes hot sauce

That's all it needs as a great basic dip, but feel free to play around with different herbs. Serve with veggies and crackers.

Spinach Dip
2 cups

1 10 oz. pkg. frozen, chopped spinach, thawed and squeezed dry
4 oz. water chestnuts, chopped fine
½ c. sour cream
½ c. plain yogurt
½ c. finely chopped green onion

¼ tsp. salt
¼ tsp. dried tarragon leaves, crushed
½ tsp. dry mustard
1 clove garlic, minced
❦ pepper, to taste

Blend all ingredients. Check salt. Chill 1-2 hours before serving.

Sweet Fruit Dressing or Dip
1 cup

½ c. whipping cream, whipped to soft folds
2 Tbs. fresh lime juice
1 Tbs. grated lime peel
2 Tbs. honey
1 tsp. minced crystallized ginger

¼ c. mayonnaise or plain yogurt

Fold all together gently. Mix with fruits and chill for salad, or use as dip for assorted fresh fruit.

Bleu Cheese Dip for Fruits
2 cups

Cream until light:
3 oz. soft cream cheese
1/3 c. mayonnaise
1 Tbs. fresh lemon juice

Fold in:
4 oz. crumbled bleu cheese
¼ tsp. salt

½ c. whipping cream, whipped to soft peaks

Chill and serve with sweet-tangy fruits, such as golden delicious apples, grapes, pears, citrus, strawberries.

Walnut Hummus with Cilantro
2½ cups

1   15 oz. can garbanzo beans, drained
½   c. walnuts
3   Tbs. garbanzo liquid reserved from can
3   Tbs. olive oil
3   Tbs. fresh lemon juice
2/3   c. cilantro leaves, semi packed down
1   clove garlic, cut, if desired

  salt, pepper, to taste

Blend all together to smooth paste in blender.

Serve as a spread or dip.

A great combination of flavors. This has been a family favorite for many years.

Tofu "Egg" Salad
Enough for 6-8 sandwiches

1   lb. tofu, smushed
½   c. mayonnaise
1/3   c. chopped dill pickles
1   stalk celery, chopped fine
2   tsp. prepared mustard
½   tsp. turmeric
½   tsp. dill weed
1   Tbs. pickle juice
  minced green pepper, or onion or both, if desired

  salt, pepper, to taste

Cream all together, beating well (can use mixer), until tofu is totally homogenized and changes texture to a smooth-and-tasty paste.

Use for sandwich filling, on crackers, cuces, celery; as a dip.

Swiss Cheese Spread with Walnuts

2½   c. grated Swiss cheese (¼ lb.)
3   Tbs. Dijon-style mustard
3   Tbs. soft cream cheese
½   c. thin sliced green onion
¼   tsp. dried tarragon
¼   tsp. pepper
½   c. crushed walnuts, lightly toasted and cooled

Cream all but walnuts together well. Mix in walnuts.

Let flavors blend overnight in fridge. Serve at room temp.

Serve with crackers or bread.

Bean Spread
1 cup

1 10 oz. can bean with bacon
   soup concentrate
4 oz. soft cream cheese
½ Tbs. Worcestershire sauce
2-3 minced green onions, or
   2-3 Tbs. white onion
3 Tbs. minced parsley

🌶 dashes hot sauce
🌶 onion, garlic powder,
   if desired

Blend well together and serve with
tortilla chips, veggies, or even Ritz
crackers.

Eggplant Caviar
2 cups

1 large eggplant
¼ c. minced cilantro, or fresh
   parsley, or half and half
3 Tbs. olive oil
2 Tbs. plain yogurt
1 Tbs. tahini
½ tsp. ground cumin
✎ salt, pepper, to taste

☺ onion and/or garlic powder,
   to taste, if desired

Score eggplant hide, oil, and bake
until soft, about 50 minutes. Cool.
Scoop out pulp and chop fine, fine,
fine. Mix well with remaining
ingredients. Serve chilled with
crackers.

Ricotta-Walnut Spread
3 cups

1   c. ricotta cheese
1 1/3 c. walnuts
1/3 c. toasted pine nuts
1/3 c. olive oil
2   Tbs. minced parsley
1   small garlic clove, cut
1   tsp. dry marjoram leaf,
    or 1 Tbs. fresh

Blend all together in food
processor or blender.

Besides being a nice spread or dip,
it can also be used tossed with hot
fettuccini noodles and Parmesan.

Stuffed Cherry Tomatoes
40-50 pieces

1 box cherry tomatoes, halved
½ recipe Herb Cheese or ½
   recipe Walnut Hummus
   with Cilantro

Scoop seeds out of tomato halves
and mound with your choice of
filling. Garnish with parsley bits.

Savories, Sauces and Tidbits

Herb Cheese
1 cup

2 Tbs. soft butter
4 oz. soft cream cheese
1 Tbs. chopped fresh thyme
   leaves, or 1 tsp. dry
1 Tbs. fresh marjoram, or
   1 tsp. dry
1 Tbs. minced parsley
½ tsp. fresh ground pepper
1 tsp. fresh lemon juice
½ c. sour cream

Whip butter and cream cheese together with herbs and lemon juice till light and fluffy. Blend in sour cream. Chill 1-2 hours.

Creamy and delicately elegant. Use a decorating tube to make a flower on a bit of bread or cracker, or vegetable.

Tangy Cheese Spread
2½ cups

6 oz. feta cheese
1 c. cottage cheese
8 oz. soft cream cheese
4 oz. bleu cheese
2 Tbs. cream
2 Tbs. white wine, or white
   grape juice
2 dashes Tabasco
♥ dash Worcestershire sauce
♥ pinch allspice

Dump in blender or processor and blend till smooth. Another good spread for French bread!

Olive Cheese Ball
2½ cups

8 oz. soft cream cheese
1 c. grated Monterey,
   Muenster, or Havarti
   cheese
2 Tbs. butter
1/3 c. sherry or red grape juice
¼ c. Parmesan cheese
1 tsp. marjoram or dill
1 6 oz. can black olives,
   drained and chopped

Combine cheeses and butter, and cream until smooth and fluffy. Mix in sherry, Parmesan and herb.

Line a small bowl as a mold, with plastic wrap. Cover inside surface with a layer of chopped olives. Mix any extra into cheese. Pack cheese into bowl, smoothing top. Cover and chill several hours. Turn over onto plate. Serve with crackers.

Fresh Tomato Sauce
3 cups
This is a light sauce that still has the fresh tomato taste. Fruity olive oil makes it sublime!

6 c. finely chopped or cubed fresh tomatoes (about 6-7)
½ c. fruity extra virgin olive oil
1 Tbs. oregano
2 tsp. marjoram
1 tsp. thyme
1/3 c. minced parsley
½ c. minced fresh basil or 1 Tbs. dried

½ green pepper, chopped fine
¼ c. minced onion, if desired
1-2 cloves garlic, minced
salt, pepper, to taste

Heat oil in heavy saucepan. (Not too hot or you will burn the herbs) Stir in herbs then green pepper, onion and garlic. Cook a few minutes and add tomatoes. Heat and simmer 15-20 minutes.

Cranberry-Raspberry Sauce
4 cups

Good with poultry
10 oz. pkg. frozen raspberries, thawed
1 c. water
1 lb. fresh cranberries
1½ c. sugar

Strain raspberries, saving juice. In large saucepan, mix juice, water, cranberries and sugar. Bring to boil. Cook until cranberries pop open. Stir in raspberries and chill.

Mango Sauce
2½ cups

1 Tbs. oil
¼ c. chopped onion
¼ c. chopped carrot
1 fresh hot chili pepper, like habanero
1 lb. bag frozen mangos chunks
½ c. white wine vinegar
¼ c. catsup
2 Tbs. packed brown sugar

Heat oil in large saucepan and cook onion, carrot and chili about 5 minutes. Stir in mango, vinegar, catsup and sugar. Heat to boiling, reduce and simmer 10 minutes, uncovered, stirring often. Cool a bit and blend in blender till smooth. Best served warm.
Use with turnovers, fried tofu, baked chicken or turkey, or fritters.

Béchamel Sauce
5 cups

Good for pouring over pasta and veggies, baking in casserole or pie

- $\frac{1}{2}$ c. butter
- $\frac{1}{2}$ c. flour
- 4 c. hot milk
- 4 eggs
- 🥕 pinch nutmeg
- 🥕 salt, pepper to taste

In large saucepan melt butter and cook flour in it, stirring constantly 5 minutes, until golden brown. Beat in hot milk gradually, whisking until smooth. In blender, beat eggs frothy and, while still running, gradually add half the sauce. Whisk back into saucepan and cook till smooth and thick. Season.

Cheese Sauce
3 cups

- 4 Tbs. butter
- 4 Tbs. flour
- $\frac{1}{2}$ tsp. dry mustard
- 🥕 salt, pepper to taste
- 🥕 pinch nutmeg
- $1\frac{3}{4}$ c. milk
- 4 oz. cream cheese
- $1\frac{1}{2}$ c. of your favorite cheese, grated

Melt butter. Whisk in flour and seasonings and cook a few minutes. Whisk in milk and cook, stirring, till thick and bubbly. Stir in cheeses, low heat, till melted and smooth.

Serve over veggies. Try puff pastry shells filled with veggies and cheese sauce. (My daughter whips this up in a flash.)

Cashew Gravy
$3\frac{1}{2}$ cups

- 1 c. raw cashews
- $2\frac{1}{2}$ c. water
- 2 Tbs. butter
- 2 Tbs. flour
- $\frac{1}{2}$ tsp. Spike seasoning salt
- $\frac{1}{2}$ tsp. rubbed sage
- 1 tsp. onion powder
- $\frac{1}{4}$ tsp. pepper
- 🥕 pinch rosemary

Blend cashews with water in blender till smooth. In saucepan heat butter over medium-low heat till melted and browned. Watch carefully that it doesn't go too far. Stir in seasonings with flour and cook several minutes. Add blended cashews and cook, stirring, till it comes to a boil and thickens. Cook a few minutes. Serve as gravy over rice, potato, veggies, and nut loaf.

Easy Savory Lemon Sauce
1 2/3 cup

1	c. mayonnaise	Whisk together well in saucepan and cook, stirring, over medium-low heat till smooth.
2	eggs	
3	Tbs. fresh lemon juice	
½	tsp. dry mustard	
½	tsp. salt	Nice sauce for veggies or Eggs Benedict.
☺	pepper to taste	

Mustard-Dill Sauce
1½ cups

2/3 c. sour cream
2/3 c. plain yogurt
¼ c. Dijon mustard
2 Tbs. fresh dill, chopped, or

2 tsp. dry
☺ salt, pepper to taste

Mix all together well, and chill. Use as dip, sauce or dressing.

Tahini-Eggplant Sauce
1½ cups

1 medium eggplant
1/3 c. sesame butter or tahini
3 Tbs. olive oil
3 Tbs. soy sauce
1 Tbs. fresh lemon juice
½ c. minced fresh cilantro
¼ tsp. garlic powder
☺ sprinkle red pepper flakes
☺ salt to taste

Score eggplant, oil and bake whole at 350° till tender, about 50 minutes. Cool and scoop out innards. Blend well with rest of ingredients.

Use as a sauce on veggies or noodles, or a dip

Balsamic Bar-B-Q Sauce
Very quick and easy. I whip it together to broil several pieces of chicken.

Mix together ½ cup catsup, about 2 Tbs. molasses and 1-2 Tbs. balsamic vinegar. Excellent tongue zapper. Play around with the proportions.

Ginger Bar-B-Q Sauce
1½ cups

½ c. soy sauce
½ c. catsup
¼ c. chicken stock or dry white wine
3 Tbs. brown sugar
2 Tbs. fresh grated ginger

Whisk together well. Use as a marinade for roasted or grilled vegetables, tofu, or flying or swimming vegetables.

Bar-B-Q Sauce
1 cup

8 oz. tomato sauce
4-6 Tbs. molasses
¼ c. apple cider vinegar, or try part balsamic vinegar
2 Tbs. Worcestershire sauce
1 Tbs. soy sauce
1 Tbs. prepared mustard
1 tsp. thyme
☺ pepper to taste

Mix well and in saucepan, bring to boil and then simmer down to a thick sauce, stirring often, about 40 minutes.

Enough to baste 1 whole chicken Double recipe for pasta with tofu balls.

Currant Sauce
1½ cups

1 c. currant sauce
½ tsp. dry mustard
2 Tbs. orange juice
2 Tbs. fresh lemon juice
2 tsp. grated lemon peel
¼ c. port or Madeira wine
2 medium shallots, peeled

Heat jelly in saucepan, low heat. Whisk in mustard and juices and zest. Cream wine and shallots in blender and add to jelly. Cook 2 minutes.

Use as a glaze on roasting chicken or turkey, or as a colorful relish. Good on corn fritters.

Pesto Sauce
1½ cups

1/3 c. extra virgin olive oil
1/3 c. Parmesan cheese,
preferably fresh grated
½ c. fresh basil leaves
¼ c. chopped parsley
¼ c. pinenuts or walnuts
1 Tbs. fresh lemon juice

1 clove garlic, peeled
1 tsp. salt
¼ tsp. pepper

Blend all in blender till smooth.
Toss with hot pasta.

Pineapple Plum Sweet-Sour Sauce
2 cups

1 8 oz. can crushed pineapple,
with juice
1/3 c. sugar
½ c. apple cider vinegar
1 Tbs. soy sauce
1 Tbs. cornstarch mixed with
1 Tbs. cold water
2/3 c. plum jam

Heat all to boiling, except plum
jam, stirring constantly, until clear
and slightly thick. Stir in plum
jam. Cool. Use as a dipping sauce
for little tasties, a sauce for rice
and veggies, on chicken, or tofu
balls.

Sweet-Sour Sauce with Mandarin Oranges
3½ cups

1 c. pineapple juice
11 oz. can mandarin oranges,
with juice
½ c. water
2-3 Tbs. rice or white vinegar
1 Tbs. sugar
½ c. catsup
1 Tbs. soy sauce

2½ Tbs. cornstarch
1 tsp. powdered ginger, or
1 Tbs. fresh grated

Mix all together and cook in
saucepan till thick. Serve hot
with tofu balls or chicken and
veggies and rice.

Salads, Relishes & Dressings

Party Salad

Got a big platter? Let's Party!
An arrangement of a large platter of healthy fresh-tasting and tangy salads, with an abundance of colors, textures, tastes and varieties is an inspiring and welcome "conversation piece"- not to mention a chance to use creative, mad-scientist, self expression, and, of course, creature satisfaction.

Make a bed of 2 or 3 different colors and varieties of lettuce or other greens (try some of that frilly endive). Arrange mounds of prepared salads and relishes. Add simple but glorious radish roses and some julienne crisp fresh vegetables such as carrots, celery, and broccoli. Add some wedges of jicama or daikon radish. Garnish even more with olives, avocado, etc.

Use salads such as: Green Bean Vinaigrette with Roasted Red Pepper, Italian Potato Salad, Feta-Ricotta Mound, Radish Relish or Italian Relish, Walnut Hummus with Cilantro. (All in index)

Set a basket of crackers near by. To make it fuller yet, include a round tray of tomatoes and cheese and a basket of French bread. How about some herb butter? Got any ideas for the rest of the menu?

Tidbit about lettuce:
I've tried the fancy lettuce crisper things and found them cumbersome and extra work. Best thing I've found is wrapping just washed lettuce in a large, clean dish cloth (Those olde flour sacks were great) and putting all in the fridge to drain and crisp. Sprinkle with a little water after a day or so.

Greek Spinach Salad

Arrange on individual salad plates:
- fresh spinach leaves, washed, dried, broken in bite sized pieces
- another leafy green, prepared as above
- grated carrot
- grated daikon or red radish
- tomato slices
- red onion slices if desired
- Greek olives
- Feta cheese, cut in cubes
- Sprinkles dried oregano

Sprinkle with Italian Dressing or Vinaigrette, or use your own favorite dressing.

Cheese and Tomato Platter

Find a round-shaped farmer's cheese or mozzarella and have it sliced sandwich thin by your friendly grocer. Find even-sized well-ripened fresh tomatoes and slice them evenly, $\frac{1}{4}$" thick. Allow 1-2 slices per person.

If the cheese round is bigger than the tomatoes, cut the cheese slices in half.

Arrange a cheese slice overlapping on top of a tomato slice, with $\frac{1}{2}$" of tomato showing on one edge. Arrange tomato-cheese pairs overlapping in a circle on a nice platter, with red edges showing in a consistent pattern. Place shallow bowl, filled with half mayo and half fancy mustard in center.

Serve with nice basket of fresh and sliced French bread.

Sweet and Tangy Fruit and Nut Salad

Use a recipe of sweet and tangy salad dressing, such as Raspberry Vinaigrette

Make a recipe of Candied Walnuts

Have prepared as much mixed salad greens as you need, such as bib lettuce, shredded red lettuce, mixed baby greens.
Toss them with the dressing and mound on serving plates.

- Crumble over top:
- choice of Blue, Roquefort,
- gorgonzola, or stilton
- cheese

- Sprinkle with candied walnuts and:
- dried cranberries

- Garnish with:
- cucumber slices
- tomato slices
- apple slices

Summer Salad
8 servings

1 lb. new potatoes
1/3 c. minced parsley
½ c. olive oil
½ lb. green beans, ½" pieces
½ lb. zucchini (2 six-inchers)
    ¼ " slices
1 head butter lettuce,
    washed, dried and chilled

Dressing:
½ c. olive oil
1/3 c. red wine vinegar
1 clove garlic, minced
☺ salt, pepper to taste

Boil or steam new potatoes till tender. Cool, peel (if desired) and cut thick slices. Mix with olive oil and parsley. Set aside. Steam green beans just tender, not soft. Cool. Steam zucchini just tender. Cool. Break lettuce into smaller pieces.

Toss all together in bowl with dressing, just wetting all surfaces without puddling dressing at bottom. Adjust salt and pepper.

Italian Relish
6-8 servings

A very nice, different taste

1 medium eggplant, cut into fingers
4 Tbs. olive oil (for sautéing)
1 cauliflower, cut in flowerettes
1 c. bouillon
1/3 c. minced parsley
¼ c. minced chives
4-5 dried tomatoes, snipped
1/3 c. pimiento or roasted red bell peppers, cut in small cubes
1/3 c. olive oil
¼ c. red wine vinegar
☺ large handful black olives, like Kalamata

1 Tbs. capers
1 tsp. oregano
☺ salt, pepper to taste

Saute eggplant in olive oil till tender. In last few minutes, add dried tomatoes and mix well. (If tomatoes are hard, soak them in hot water until soft)

Simmer cauliflower in bouillon till just tender but not mushy.

When all is cool, mix with rest of ingredients. Chill several hours.

Serve at room temperature.

Mexican Relish
3½ cups

This has a fresh, lively taste

1   recipe Fresh Mexican Salsa

Add:
1   6" zucchini, cubed and lightly steamed

1   c. fresh or frozen corn
1   red bell pepper, roasted, peeled and cubed
½   c. sliced green olives
2   Tbs. olive oil

Let set an hour, and serve.

Bean Relish
6-8 servings

Mix all together:
1   15 oz. can garbanzo beans, drained
1   15 oz. can kidney beans, drained
1½   cucumbers, peeled, seeded, chopped in small cubes
½   small red pepper, cut in small cubes
½   small green pepper, ditto

1   tomato, cut in small cubes
½   c. fresh cilantro, chopped

Dress with Vinaigrette or Italian Dressing or Honey-Mustard.

Try more:
- minced onion
- sliced olives
- cubed jicama

Trade Fair Pasta Salad
8 servings
A well loved salad that always sold in those days of yore at the Student Union Saturday Trade Fair

8   oz. rigatoni noodles (the big, wide ones), cooked, drained and rinsed
1   15 oz. can baby corn, halved lengthwise
1   c. black olives, drained
½   red sweet pepper, cut in thin strips
1   small bunch broccoli, cut on a slant and steamed

1   8 oz. can kidney beans, drained, or garbanzos
1½   c. Vegetable Vinaigrette dressing

Mix all together well and let stand at room temperature for an hour to blend flavors

Potato Salad, American Style
6-8 servings

2 lb. potatoes (6 medium), cooked, cooled, peeled, and cut into 1" cubes.
¾ c. fine chopped dill pickles
½ c. fine chopped stuffed green olives
3-4 stalks celery (not the outside ones), chopped small

½-2/3c. mayonnaise
1 Tbs. prepared yellow mustard
2-3 Tbs. pickle juice
1 tsp. onion powder
½ tsp. pepper
☺ salt to taste

Mix all together well and chill.

Italian Potato Salad
6-8 servings
When fullness meets fullness, the sun shines! And that magical something happens with fresh cooked potatoes and extra virgin olive oil

2 lbs. new potatoes or small red potatoes
1 c. of the best extra virgin olive oil
1/3 c. red wine vinegar
½ c. chopped fresh basil
2 medium fresh tomatoes, sliced, with all it's juices
☺ salt, pepper to taste
☹ black olives as garnish

Boil the potatoes in their jackets. Drain, and while still warm but not too hot to handle, peel (if desired- I don't, unless the skin comes off on its own), and slice thickly. Toss gently with olive oil and marinade at room temp for an hour.

Mix all together and serve.

Southern Potato Salad
8-10 servings
I made this at a little greasy spoon in Taos where I worked on weekends. I didn't like bread n butter pickles until I tasted them in this salad.

6 medium red potatoes
5 hard boiled eggs, sliced
1 medium Vidalia sweet onion, chopped small
1 c. bread n butter pickles, chopped (I stack them and cut them 4x4)
3 Tbs. pickle juice
1 c. mayonnaise

2 Tbs. Dijon mustard
¼ tsp. pepper
☺ salt to taste

Cook potatoes tender. Cool. (Unless you like mushy potatoes, then cut them warm.) Cut in 1½" cubes. Mix all together.

Gazpacho Potato Salad
6-8 servings

4 medium potatoes, cooked cut in 1" cubes
½ c. olive oil
1/3 c. apple cider vinegar
2 tsp. chili powder
½ tsp. seasoned salt, such as .....Spike!
½ tsp. hot pepper flakes
2 large tomatoes, coarse chopped
1 c. defrosted frozen or fresh corn
½ c. minced celery

½ c. grated carrot
½ c. ripe olives
½ c. minced parsley or cilantro
¼ c. minced green or red pepper
¼ c. minced onion

Mix seasonings and vinegar together and whisk in oil at a steady stream to emulsify. Mix with potatoes and rest. Chill before serving.

Vegetable Vinaigrette
6 servings

2 lbs. asparagus or green beans or cauliflower or zucchini, or combination

Simmer, covered, in 1 c. water with 1 bouillon cube, till tender-crisp. Drain. Drink juice- yum.

Whip together:
½ c. olive oil
¼ c. other vegetable oil
½ c. apple cider vinegar

4 tsp. Dijon mustard
1 tsp. salt
¼ tsp. pepper
2-3 Tbs. minced parsley

Whisk together seasonings and vinegar. Add oil in steady stream, whisking, to emulsify.
Mix with veggies and let stand at room temp 2 hours. Garnish with tomato or olive.

Green Bean Vinaigrette with Roasted Red Pepper

Follow recipe for Vegetable Vinaigrette, using green beans.

Roast 2 red sweet peppers (as in Pablano Chiles in Cream)

Cut out tops and inside ribs of roasted pepper; wash out seeds. Cut peppers in 2"-3" long thin strips. Toss with green beans and marinade. Add a few black olives.

Swiss Potato and Green Bean Salad
5-6 servings

½ lb. green beans, whole
2 medium potatoes, cut lengthwise and sliced thin
¼ c. fresh lemon juice
1 Tbs. apple cider vinegar
½ c. olive oil
1 tsp. Dijon mustard
½ tsp. crushed tarragon
½ tsp. dill
½ tsp. salt
¼ tsp. pepper
½ lb. Swiss cheese, thin strips
1/3 c. broken black olives

Steam beans till just tender. Place in mixing bowl. Steam potatoes till tender and add to beans.

In small bowl, whisk all the herbs and seasonings together with lemon juice, vinegar and oil. Combine with rest and toss to blend well. Let marinate several hours, covered, in fridge.

Chicken Salad with Feta Cheese and Cilantro
4-6 servings

2 c. cubed cooked chicken breasts (about 3)
2 c. peeled, cubed cucumber
2/3 c. sliced black olives
¼ c. minced fresh cilantro
1 c. ½" cubes Feta cheese
1 clove garlic, minced
½ c. mayonnaise
½ c. plain yogurt

2 tsp. oregano
1 tsp. ground cumin, roasted
½ tsp. salt
¼ tsp. pepper

Mix all together and chill. Serve on butter lettuce and spinach. Or in whole-wheat pita bread with shredded romaine.

Tortellini Salad with Creamy Dijon Dressing
6-8 servings

8 oz. fresh or frozen stuffed tortellini, cooked, drained
3 stalks celery, chopped fine
1/3 c. minced dried tomato preserved in olive oil
1 small cucumber, peeled, chopped

1 c. radishes, chopped
1 fresh tomato, sliced, if desired
¼ c. minced parsley
2 Tbs. minced fresh basil

Toss with Creamy Dijon Dressing. Serve chilled.

Pineapple-Chicken Salad
6-8 servings

4 chicken breasts
 rosemary, tarragon
2 green onions, minced
½ small red onion, minced
1 small stalk celery, chopped
 small
1 8 oz. can juice sweetened
 pineapple chunks, drained
½ c. mayonnaise
1½ Tbs. Dijon mustard
 salt, pepper to taste

Poach (barely simmer at low heat) breasts in barely enough water to cover with pinches of rosemary and tarragon, until just turned white from pink, about 15 minutes...Cool and cut in bite-size cubes. (Use broth for something else)

Combine all ingredients and chill, adjusting seasoning.

Caesar Salad with Dried Tomato Vinaigrette
4-6 servings

3-4 heads romaine
1 recipe Dried Tomato
 Vinaigrette

Croutons:
2 Tbs. butter
2 Tbs. olive oil
2 cloves garlic, chopped
 salt, pepper to taste
3 c. ¾" cubes French bread

In small saucepan, melt butter, oil, garlic, salt and pepper and stir a bit. In a bowl, toss bread cubes with oil as you drizzle it on. Spread on cookie sheet and bake 12-15 minutes at 350°, until golden. Set aside.

Make dressing.

Use only the paler, inner leaves of washed and dried lettuce. Tear into bite-size pieces, about 12 cups.

Just before serving, toss lettuce and croutons with dressing in a large bowl. Garnish with more parmesan.

Tabbouleh
6-8 servings

1   c. cracked bulghur wheat
1/3   c. olive oil
2/3   c. fresh lemon juice
2   bunch parsley, minced
3   large tomatoes, chopped
fine
1   large cucumber, ditto
2   celery ribs, ditto
6   green olives, ditto
✎   salt, pepper to taste

Soak bulghur in boiling water a half hour, until tender. Drain well.

Mix with all ingredients and chill, covered, 2-25 hours (over-night is best). To serve, spoon onto leaf lettuce arranged on platter or individual plates.

Spiced Olives
3 cups

I have a fond memory as a kid of driving out with my dad to the Mojave Desert and bringing back a gallon of locally grown, cured green olives. They were in brine and good as they were. But then he would mix in a whole head of garlic, separated and peeled of course, and store them in a cupboard under the sink. I would sneak in and grab a handful and head for the great outdoors to eat my prize in peace. Wonderful! I never "got caught", but they must have wondered or maybe were just being nice. Then, after college, in my hippie days, I lived up above Santa Barbara in an old olive grove planted by the Spaniards over 100 years before (more now). I didn't camp out. I lived in a cute little playhouse built for the children of the owners of the estate I was on. (The children had grown up and moved on, but that is another story.) I couldn't resist those olive laden trees and tried my hand at curing large tubs of olives. It is a process, curing them in lye. But they came out very well and I stored the cured olives in olive oil and herbs and gave them away as Christmas presents. Friends were thrilled. So here's a sample. Not homemade, but still great.

1   15 oz. can black olives,
or a fancy olive-Kalamata
1   7 oz. jar green, stuffed
olives, drained
½   c. cider vinegar
1   c. olive oil
2-3   cloves garlic, peeled,
sliced
2   tsp. oregano

If olives are unpitted, split them slightly. Place in quart jar with remaining ingredients. Cover tightly and shake. Marinate overnight. Serve at room temperature.

Serve as a relish.

Feta-Ricotta Cheese Salad
6 servings

6 oz. feta cheese
½ c. ricotta cheese
1 Tbs. fresh lemon juice
♥ generous sprinkle fresh black pepper

6 red lettuce or butter lettuce leaves, washed and dried
1 large tomato, sliced in thin wedges
1 ripe avocado, peeled and sliced lengthwise
♥ large handful Greek olives
♥ olive oil
♥ favorite salad dressing

Crumble feta with fingers into a small bowl. Mix in ricotta, lemon juice and pepper. Shape into a ball and place on serving platter lined with lettuce leaves. Arrange around cheese the tomatoes and avocados, in a pleasing petal pattern, with olives. Sprinkle olive oil on cheese ball. Sprinkle dressing on veggies.

Serve with crusty French bread, whose presence will help spread cheese and good cheer. Or can serve on that party platter with other good flavors.

Quinoa Salad with Tomato and Roasted Shallots
4 servings

Quinoa is a tasty grain and adds a refreshing change of pace. Or try this recipe with garbanzo beans.

1 c. quinoa
2 c. chicken or vegetable bouillon
6 shallots, peeled and halved lengthwise
1 large, juicy tomato, chopped large
2 Tbs. minced parsley
½ c. olive oil
3 Tbs. red wine vinegar or sherry vinegar
2 cloves garlic, minced
1 green onion, minced
½ tsp. dry mustard
❧ salt, pepper
❧ kalamata olives, garnish

Using a fine mesh strainer, rinse quinoa under cold running water until water runs clear. Otherwise it cooks with a bitter tang. Add the grain to boiling bouillon and cook till tender, covered, 15 minutes, lowering heat. (Will still be a bit chewy). Set aside.

Oil shallots and bake in oven at 325° for 45 minutes, until tender. Cool and chop and add to quinoa, tomato and parsley in bowl. Save roasting oil.

Mix vinegar, garlic, mustard, salt, and pepper in bowl. Add oil in a thin stream, whisking to emulsify. Add roasting oil. Pour over quinoa and mix well.

Waldorf Salad of India
6 servings

Prepare:
- 2 c. peeled, diced apples
- 1 c. diced celery
- 1 c. seedless grapes, halved
- ½ c. chopped walnuts or pecans

Mix with:
- ¾ c. plain yogurt
- 2 Tbs. honey
- 1-2 tsp. rose water
- 1/8-¼ tsp. cardamom, or to taste

Chill and serve

Radish Roses and Green Onion Pom-Poms

Have you seen in the grocery store those cheap plastic-handled, very thin bladed little paring knives? Well grab a few-they are invaluable, without paying hardly anything. And when new and sharp or old and sharpened, they are the next best thing to a razor blade-for small precision work, such as radish roses

For radish rose: Slice radishes, either lengthwise or widthwise, in as many thin leaves as you can manage, without cutting quite all the way thru. Stop there or make a chrysanthemum: Turn the radish a quarter turn and cut leaves again at a right angle, thus making little sticks.

Place both aspiring flower types in a bowl of water laced with ice cubes and set in fridge several hours. The radishes swell and stretch to their greater glory.

For onions: Slice thin, length- wise strips on both ends, leaving an inch or two uncut in the middle. Turn a quarter turn and make more cuts. Then frill them out in ice water, just like the radish roses. Now decorate!

Fresh Mexican Salsa
1½ cups

- 1 onion, chopped fine
- 3 tomatoes, chopped small
- 1 clove garlic, minced
- 1-2 fresh serrano or jalapeno pepper, minced (don't forget your rubber gloves!)

- 2 Tbs. fresh lime juice
- ¾ c. fresh cilantro, minced
- ½ tsp. salt

Combine and chill ½ hour. Use right away.

Raisin-Nut Chutney

¾ cups

Very good stuff. Nice buzz to the taste buds.

1	c. raisins	
¼	c. raw cashew pieces	
¼	c. blanched, chopped almonds	
¼	c. pine nuts	
2	Tbs. ghee or butter	
½	tsp. salt	
½	tsp. cumin powder	
½	tsp. turmeric	
1/8	tsp. cayenne	

Pour boiling water over the raisins and nuts and soak for an hour or so, till raisins are plumped. Drain well.

Heat ghee and seasonings. Mix in raisins and nuts and cook till heated thru. Serve hot.

Radish Relish

2½ cups

My grandma had this recipe published in the Minneapolis city newspaper 60 years ago when local farmers had a bumper crop of radishes and bets were on for new ways to fix them.

1   lb. radishes (2 bunches), grated or ground coarse in food processor
3   Tbs. apple cider vinegar
4   Tbs. vegetable oil
☺   salt and pepper to taste

Mix all together and chill.

Vinegar and oil cuts the heat on spicy radishes and makes them tasty.

Fresh Cilantro-Ginger Chutney

2 cups

½   c. cucumber, peeled, split and seeded
½   tomato, large chunks
1   c. cilantro leaves
1   3" piece ginger, peeled and cut in pieces
2   Tbs. fresh lime or lemon juice
1   tsp. salt

Blend all together in blender or food processor. Serve chilled.

Tomato Raita
2 cups

Blend in mixing bowl:
- 1 c. plain yogurt
- 1 large tomato, chopped fine (can blanch the skin off first if desired, by dropping in boiling water 1 minute and rinsing and peeling)
- ½ c. shredded coconut
- 1 Tbs. minced hot chili pepper (gloves!)
- ½ tsp. salt

Heat till seeds pop:
- 1 tsp. oil
- 1 tsp. black mustard seeds
- 1 tsp. whole cumin

Stir in:
- ¼ tsp. red pepper flakes

Mix all together and chill.

Yogurt Cheese and Cucumber
2 cups

- 2 c. (16 oz.) plain yogurt
- 1 large cucumber, peeled, seed center scooped out, grated
- 2 Tbs. minced parsley
- 2 Tbs. olive oil
- 1 Tbs. white vinegar or rice vinegar
- 1 tsp. dill
- 1 clove garlic, minced, if like
- salt, pepper to taste

Use a yogurt cheese funnel, or line a strainer with cheesecloth, thin towel or coffee filter. Fill with yogurt and allow to drain, covered, in fridge, 24 hours.

Combine all ingredients in bowl with yogurt cheese and refrigerate at least 2 hours.

Apple Chutney
2 cups

- 4 c. peeled, chopped apples
- ½ c. golden raisins
- ½ c. minced onion
- ½ c. water
- ¼ c. apple juice concentrate
- ¼ c. apple cider vinegar
- 1 tsp. salt
- 1 tsp. ground coriander

- 2 Tbs. minced fresh ginger
- 1½ tsp. black mustard seed
- 6 cloves

Mix all together and simmer, uncovered, stirring often, for 1 hour. Add more juice or water, if needed.

Cranberry Chutney
5 cups

1   12 oz. bag fresh cranberries
2   whole oranges
1   small onion
2   Tbs. grated fresh ginger
¼   c. minced figs or golden
     raisins
¼   c. pine nuts, or fine
     chopped walnuts
1½   c. sugar
½   tsp. cinnamon
½   tsp. dry mustard
½   tsp. salt
¼   tsp. red pepper flakes

Either chop oranges and onion fine, or process together in food processor, in which case you can add ginger, too. (Take out seeds)

Mix all together in heavy pot and cook over medium heat, stirring frequently to prevent bottom sticking. Cook about 20-30 minutes, till cranberries are popped and sauce is bubbly. Store in fridge or freeze part of it.

Ginger Pear Pickle
6-8 servings

Serve as a fancy side to a holiday dinner. How about all those indigenous, crunchy pears, lying around at harvest time - these can be canned.

7   medium pears, peeled,
     cored, and quartered
2   c. water
1   Tbs. white vinegar

2½   c. sugar
1½   c. white vinegar
1   c. apple juice
½   c. thinly sliced, peeled
     fresh ginger
1   lime, sliced thinly
3   cinnamon sticks
2   Tbs. whole cloves

Combine pears, water and 2 Tbs. vinegar in bowl and let stand 10 minutes.

Combine sugar, vinegar, juice, ginger, and lime in saucepan and bring to a boil over high heat. Add spices tied in a cheesecloth or tea ball. Cover and boil 8-10 minutes.

Drain pears well and add to sugar syrup and boil about 10 minutes, until pears are translucent. Cool, and then chill before serving.

Dressings

All recipes containing olive oil are Extra Virgin olive oil, unless otherwise stated.
It has the most flavor and is the least processed

Italian Dressing
1½ cups

1	c. olive oil
¼	c. fresh lemon juice
¼	c. wine or cider vinegar
1	tsp. oregano
½	tsp. dry mustard
½	tsp. onion powder
½	tsp. paprika
1/8	tsp. thyme

2	cloves garlic, crushed
1	tsp. salt
1	tsp. sugar
¼	tsp. pepper

Whisk all together but olive oil.
Add olive oil in a thin stream,
whisking well to emulsify. Chill.

Vinaigrette Dressing
1½ cups

½	c. cider vinegar
½	c. olive oil
½	c. other vegetable oil
4	Tsp. Dijon mustard
1	tsp. salt
¼	tsp. pepper

2	Tbs. grated green pepper, if desired
2-3	Tbs. minced parsley

Whisk all together except oils.
Add those in thin stream while
whisking, to emulsify. Chill.

Creamy Dijon Dressing
1 cup

Whip together:

3	Tbs. mayonnaise
1	Tbs. Dijon mustard
1	tsp. honey
1	tsp. salt
½	tsp. pepper

1	large clove garlic, crushed, if desired

Add in a thin stream, whisking:

½	c. olive oil

Green Dressing
2 cups

Mix in blender till smooth:

1½	c. mayonnaise
¼	c. cider vinegar or fresh lemon juice
½	bunch washed spinach

½	bunch fresh parsley
½	tsp. celery seed
½	tsp. salt
¼	tsp. pepper

Buttermilk-Roquefort Dressing
2 cups

¾ c. buttermilk
½ c. olive oil
1/3 c. packed chives or green onion (or try parsley)
¼ lb. Roquefort cheese, or Bleu cheese

In food processor or blender, add buttermilk, oil, greens and half the cheese. Blend till smooth. Add remaining cheese and blend a few seconds, so still a bit lumpy.

French Dressing
1 cup

½ c. olive oil
¼ c. other vegetable oil
¼ c. cider vinegar
1 tsp. paprika
1 tsp. dry mustard
1 tsp. sugar
1 tsp. salt
¼ tsp. pepper

Whisk all together except oils. Add those in a thin stream while whisking away. Chill.

Lemon Honey Dressing
1 cup

2 sm. green onions
¼ c. fresh lemon juice
1 tsp. dry mustard
¼ c. honey
1/3 c. olive oil
♥ salt, pepper to taste

Blend onions, lemon juice and mustard in blender. Add honey in a stream and then oil, until well blended. Season to taste with salt and pepper.

Serve with avocado, grapefruit and lettuce salad.

Easy Tahini Dressing
¾ cup

3 Tbs. tahini
3 Tbs. olive oil
2-3 Tbs. lemon juice
2 Tbs. plain yogurt
2 Tbs. water
2 tsp. tamari or soy sauce

Cream all together well. Chill and serve.

Dried Tomato Vinaigrette
2/3 cup, one salad

2   olive oil packed dried tomatoes
1/3 c. parmesan
3   cloves garlic, cut up
2   tsp. red wine vinegar or sherry vinegar
2   tsp. fresh lemon juice
1   tsp. Worcestershire sauce
½   tsp. dry mustard
½   c. olive oil

Place all but olive oil in blender and blend till smooth. While whizzing, add oil in a thin stream to blend. Transfer to a bowl or toss with salad right away

Raspberry Vinaigrette
1¼ cups

½   c. olive oil
¼   c. vegetable oil
¼   c. raspberry jam
3   Tbs. apple cider vinegar
1   Tbs. balsamic vinegar
1   Tbs. Dijon mustard
½   tsp. salt
½   tsp. packed fresh oregano, or ¼ tsp. dry
½   tsp. packed fresh rosemary, or ¼ tsp. dry
¼   tsp. pepper

Add all ingredients to blender but oil and blend a few minutes. Add oil in a thin stream and blend until it emulsifies. Adjust salt and pepper.

Honey Mustard Dressing
1½ cups

2   Tbs. Dijon mustard
3   Tbs. honey
1   tsp. peeled grated fresh ginger
¼   c. apple cider vinegar
2   tsp. soy sauce
1   large garlic clove, minced and mashed to paste with
1   c.+ 2 Tbs. vegetable oil
2   Tbs. minced chive or green onion

½   tsp. salt
    pepper to taste

In a bowl, whisk together mustard, honey, ginger, vinegar, soy sauce and garlic. Add oil in a stream, whisking dressing until it is emulsified.

Stir in chives; adjust salt and pepper.

Soup

Ham Hock and Lentils

Granpa Fritz came to live with us when I was 16 and he was 75. He drove out to La Puente, California, from Minneapolis, Minnesota, in his run down old car and homemade trailer piled high with belongings, and pulled into the driveway of our home without much ado (the car and trailer were ado enough!)

I took many journeys with him in that car – journeys that lasted a lifetime the whole 4 miles to town and back. Granpa drove about 15 miles an hour and wandered from side to side on the road. I would look back in dismay– and from as low a vantage point as possible– at the long line of cars behind us. Of course, Granpa was fine. He was also good for lots of stories. Only, in his thick German accent, I didn't always catch all the nuances.

Many times I would come home from school to a pot of lentils, cooked long and diligently with a big ham hock for flavor. It was an impressive sight, smell and taste, with tender ham flaking into buttery melted lentils.

In later years, it was my great joy to find a vegetable substitute for ham hocks– olive oil! Again, that magical something happens, this time when primo, extra virgin olive oil meets beans! It was **Greekish Lentil Soup** that presented that particular revelation. It also happens with olive oil and potatoes, as in **Italian Potato Salad.**

Greekish Lentil Soup
6-8 servings

Simmer until tender 2-3 hours, covered:
- 2 c. lentils, soaked overnight, rinsed and drained
- 3 qts. stock or water

Add and simmer 30 minutes, till tender
- 1 stalk celery, chopped fine
- 1 carrot, chopped in cubes
- 1 medium potato, chopped

- ½ c. olive oil
- 2/3 c. tomato sauce
- ½ c. parsley
- 1 medium onion, chopped small
- ½ tsp. garlic powder
- ✐ salt, pepper to taste

Add more stock, if needed, during the simmering process. Season to taste.

Peasant Soup
6-8 servings
Succulent and satisfying - the same magic happens here with olive oil.

- 2 c. great northern beans, or navy, soaked overnight, drained and rinsed
- 2 qts. water or stock
- 3 carrots, thinly sliced
- 2 stalks celery, thinly sliced
- 1 large onion, chopped
- 2 cloves garlic, minced
- 1 16 oz. can tomatoes, crushed, or 1 lb. fresh tomatoes, chopped

- ½ c. olive oil
- 2 bay leaves
- ☺ salt, pepper to taste

Add water or stock (or bouillon) to beans in large pot. Bring to a boil and simmer 1½-2 hours, till tender. Add rest, and, partially covered, simmer about 45 minutes, till tender and melting.

Tidbit about sticky pots: It sometimes happens when we heat a pot of soup, stew or sauce of some kind that the bottom of the pot will stick and even start to burn. Just turn the heat off and put the top on the pot. Wait five minutes or so and find the bottom magically unstuck, unless, of course, it is tragically burnt. Even then, don't despair. Clean and boil the burnt pot with water and baking soda 10 minutes. It froths so don't fill it too full. Scrub and repeat, if necessary. It works!

Frijole Soup
4-6 servings

Cook together 2-3 hours until mushy tender and water cooks down:
- 1 lb. pinto beans, soaked over night and drained
- 4 qts. water

Saute in 4 Tbs. olive oil 5 minutes and add to beans:
- ½ c. tomato sauce
- 2 tsp. oregano

- 2 tsp. cumin powder
- 1 tsp. marjoram
- 2 tsp. onion powder

Put beans thru blender till smooth, or mash with masher

Add and simmer 15 minutes:
- ¼ c. chopped cilantro
- ☺ salt, pepper to taste

Broccoli Leek Soup with Watercress
4-6 servings

- 2 sm. leeks, trimmed and chopped
- 1 small onion, chopped
- 1 tsp. fresh rosemary or ½ tsp. dry
- 1/3 c. butter
- 1 potato, chopped
- 4-5 c. broth or bouillon
- 1 bunch broccoli, trimmed and chopped
- 1 bunch watercress, rinsed and stemmed
- ½ c. heavy cream
- ✎ salt, pepper to taste

Cut leeks in half lengthwise and wash insides well before chopping (sand). Saute leeks, onion and rosemary in butter about 15 minutes, on low.

Add potato and broth and simmer, uncovered, another 15 minutes. Add broccoli and cook until tender, covered, about 12 minutes.

Remove from heat and add watercress. Let stand, covered, 5 minutes. Blend in blender till smooth. Return to pan and reheat with cream, adding salt and pepper.

Bean Stew Portugal
6-8 servings
A very nice friend whose family is Portuguese served this to us one night

1   c. dry red beans, or pinto
1   medium potato, chopped
1   medium carrot, chopped
½   c. olive oil
1   large onion, cut small
2   large cloves garlic, minced
2   hefty c. chopped tomatoes
1   c. chopped stuffed green
    olives
½   c. red wine
1   tsp. cumin
2   tsp. marjoram
☺   pepper to taste

Soak beans overnight. Drain, rinse and refill large pot with water. Cook beans 1½-2 hours until tender, adding more boiling water as needed to keep them saucy. For last half hour of cooking add potato and carrot and cook till all is tender.

In hot oil, saute onions and garlic 5 minutes. Add seasonings and stir. Add tomatoes and olives and wine and simmer 10 minutes. Mix with beans and cook 10 minutes more.

Barley Stew
6-8 servings

2   Tbs. olive oil
½   lb. pearl onions, blanched
    and peeled
1   tsp. oregano
1   tsp. marjoram
2   cloves garlic, minced
1   16 oz. can tomatoes,
    chopped, with juice
6   c. chicken or veg bouillon
½   c. pearl barley
½   lb. green beans, halved
½   lb. broad beans, 1" pieces
    (if you can find them, they
    are wonderful. Or a sub.)
1   medium potato, cut in half,
    lengthwise and sliced thin

1   16 oz can artichoke hearts,
    cut in quarters
1   medium fennel bulb, sliced
⚐   salt, pepper to taste

Saute onions in oil till they start to wilt. Add garlic and herbs and cook a few minutes. Add tomatoes and stock and bring to boil. Lower heat and simmer 10 minutes, uncovered. Add barley, cover, reduce heat and cook, stirring occasionally, 20 minutes.

Add vegetables and cook until tender, 15-20 minutes. Add salt and pepper, to taste.

Green Chile Soup
4-5 servings

Spicily delicious!

2	Tbs. olive oil
1	Tbs. butter
1	tsp. paprika
1	tsp. oregano
½	tsp. marjoram
½	tsp. cumin
1	tsp. salt
¼	tsp. hot pepper flakes
¾	c. chopped green onions
1-2	cloves garlic, peeled, sliced
1	lb. (2) tomatoes, wedges
1	medium potato, cubed
1	4 oz. can chopped green chilies
½	c. corn kernels
2	Tbs. chopped cilantro
6½	c. chicken stock or veggie bouillon

Heat oil and butter and add herbs, onion and garlic. Cook 5 minutes, stirring. Blend tomatoes in blender just enough to chop them up and make half of them pureed. Add tomatoes, veggies and broth to onions and bring to boil. Simmer till potatoes are tender, 30 minutes.

To serve with cheese:
Ladle hot soup over small cheese chunks in individual soup bowls.

To serve with chicken:
Poach 1-2 chicken breasts in just a little water, covered, on low heat- a bare simmer- until it just looses it's pink. Cool, bone, cut in chunks. Add to soup with broth 5 minutes before serving.

French Onion Soup
6-8 servings

4	large onions, peeled, cut in half, lengthwise and sliced very thin
½	c. butter
1	stalk celery, minced
¼	c. minced parsley
½	c. dry white wine or sherry
6	c. chicken broth, or veggie
✐	pepper, salt

Saute onions and celery in butter till they are limpish and transparent and just browning on bottom of the pot. Add stock, wine and seasonings and bring to boil. Then simmer 10 minutes.

Serve French style in individual ovenproof bowls with toasted French bread on top sprinkled with Swiss or Gruyere or Parmesan and broiled a few minutes till bubbly.

Serve Jewish style by adding poached chicken (as in above recipe) with 1 c. cooked rice.

Go-with-the-Flow Minestrone Soup
8-10 servings

This means you can use up all those odds and ends in your fridge.

Saute a few minutes in hot oil:
- 4 Tbs. olive oil
- 2 tsp. Spike seasoning salt
- 1 tsp. dry basil or 2 Tbs. fresh
- 1 tsp. oregano
- 1 tsp. marjoram
- ½ tsp. paprika

Add and brown for 10 minutes:
- 1 small onion, chopped, if desired
- 2 carrots, cut in fingers
- 2 potatoes, cubed large
- 1 stalk celery, thin slices

Add to pot:
- 1 c. green beans, halved
- 2 small zucchini, sliced
- 6 c. stock of some kind
- 1 28 oz. can tomatoes with juice, cut up
- 1 16 oz. can kidney beans, or other, with juice

Bring to a boil and add:
- ½ c. dried pasta, your choice

Simmer 10 minutes and add:
- 1 c. frozen peas

Heat 10 minutes more and serve.

Borscht
6-8 servings

A hearty soup "rooted" in flavor

- ☺ tops from 4 beets- stack leaves, cut down middle and cut into ½" pieces
- 4 large beets
- 1 large potato, boiled, cubed
- 4 c. water, including strained beet cooking water
- 1 c. grated carrot
- 2 Tbs. butter
- 1 c. water mixed with 1 Tbs. flour
- 4 bouillon cubes or 4 tsp. granules
- 1 tsp. onion powder
- 1 Tbs. red wine vinegar
- ✐ salt, pepper to taste
- ♥ sour cream garnish

Boil the beets whole, leaving an inch on the stem end. Takes about 45-55 minutes till they are tender. Trim off root and stem ends and slip off skin with fingers. Cube.

Simmer beets in stock with butter, onion and carrots for 10 minutes.

Add flour, water and rest, including beet tops, and simmer 10 minutes. Adjust salt and pepper. Serve with dollops of sour cream

East-West Dahl Stew
8-12 servings
This was another Trade Fair favorite.

1 lb. split peas, or dahl of your choice
10 c. water or stock
3 medium potatoes, cut in large cubes
2 medium carrots, cubed
3 medium zucchinis, sliced
2 bay leaves
4 Tbs. butter or ghee

Mix all together:
3 tsp. ground cumin
2 tsp. black mustard seed
2 tsp. ground coriander
2 tsp. powdered ginger
1-2 tsp. Spike seasoning salt
1 tsp. turmeric
1½ tsp. garam masala or pumpkin pie spice mix
☺ pinch fennel seed
✎ salt, pepper, cayenne to taste

Bring peas to a boil in large pot. Add bay leaves. Cover and simmer at low heat for 1-1½ hours, stirring occasionally. Add potatoes and carrots and cook 15 minutes. Add zucchini.

Heat butter in pan and stir in mixed spices. Cook and stir a few minutes. Add to soup, getting every last bit of spice out of the pan and into the pot.

Cover and simmer 15 minutes, stirring often, until veggies are tender.

Eggplant-Dahl Stew
4 servings
A satisfying and unusual nutty flavor

Brown together in soup pot until mustard seeds start popping:
2 Tbs. oil
1 Tbs. butter
¾ c. red lentils
1 Tbs. grated fresh ginger
2 Tsp. ground cumin
2 tsp. ground coriander
2 tsp. black mustard seed

Add:
2 medium small potatoes, chopped small
1 small eggplant, chopped
1 small zucchini, chopped
4 c. water

Bring to a boil. lower the heat, cover and simmer 20-30 minutes, until thick and tender.

Mexican Turkey Meatball Soup
Serves 4-6

A very savory, delicious soup - don't skimp on the eggs, as they make the meatballs light and tender.

Saute in 3-4 Tbs. olive oil for 10 minutes:
- 2 tsp. Spike
- 1 large carrot, chopped in small chunks
- 1 medium onion, finely chopped
- 1 stalk celery, chopped small

Add to veggies in pot:
- 6 c. chicken stock or water with bouillon
- 6 Tbs. tomato sauce
- ¼ tsp. pepper

For meatballs, mix together well:
- 1 pound ground turkey
- ¼ c. uncooked rice
- 2 eggs
- 2 Tbs. minced parsley
- ½ tsp. dry roasted cumin powder, or
- 1 tsp. dry roasted whole cumin seed
- ¼ tsp. whole oregano
- ½ tsp. salt
- ☺ pinch cayenne

Bring stock and veggies to a boil and drop turkey into stock by forming a ball on a teaspoon and slipping it off the spoon into the stock.

Add a large handful of green beans, cut in short pieces

Lower heat and simmer 20-25 minutes.

Last 5 minutes of cooking, add to soup:
- ½ c. fine chopped cilantro
- 1 whole fresh ear of corn, sliced in 1" rounds.

Quick and Easy Spicy Black Bean Soup with or without Turkey Sausage
4 servings

2   15 oz. cans black beans, whole, refried or one of each
2   Tbs. olive oil
1   onion, diced
3   cloves garlic, minced
1   tsp. ground cumin
1-2 chipotle peppers, minced (from a can of Chipotle Peppers in Adobo Sauce)
1   bay leaf
3   c. chicken stock or bouillon
6-8 oz. turkey sausage, diced, if desired
☺   salt to taste
2   Tbs. minced fresh cilantro

Heat olive oil in saucepan over low heat and saute onions and garlic 4-5 minutes, with cumin.

If using all whole beans, add one can to pot and mash with potato masher. Add rest of beans with chipotle pepper and bay leaf. Mix well.

Stir in stock and turkey; bring to a boil, turn down and simmer, covered 5 minutes, till heated thru. Salt to taste.

Stir in cilantro and serve.

Easy Corn Chowder
6-8 servings

2   small potatoes, cubed and cooked
1   16 oz. bag frozen corn, defrosted
1   qt. half & half cream
2   Tbs. flour
¼   c. butter
1   tsp. oregano
½   tsp. onion powder
1   pinch each, marjoram, and thyme
1/3 c. minced parsley
✎   salt, pepper to taste

Blend 2/3 of corn with the half & half and flour in the blender, till smooth. Melt butter in saucepan and stir in seasonings. Add blended and whole corn, potato and parsley.

Heat gently, stirring often, until hot. Don't boil, just simmer a little.

Turkey and Cabbage Pottage
6 servings

Brown in soup pot over medium heat:

3	Tbs. olive oil
1	lb. ground turkey
1	large onion, chopped fine
3	cloves garlic, minced
2	tsp. chili powder mix
☺	tsp. cumin seed, toasted
1	tsp. thyme
2	bay leaves

Add to the pot and bring to a boil:

¼	c. tomato sauce
1	c. white wine

Cook until the liquid is reduced by half.

Add to pot:

4	c. stock or bouillon
8	c. cabbage, chopped
2	c. potatoes, 1 inch pieces
1	carrot, chopped
☺	salt and pepper to taste

Bring to a boil, then lower heat and simmer till veggies are tender. Adjust seasonings.

Creamy Carrot Soup
Serves 6-8

3	Tbs. butter
1	tsp. ground cumin
1	tsp. ground coriander
1	Tbs. grated fresh ginger
5-6	c. chopped carrots (about 2 pounds)
2	medium onions, chopped
2	potatoes, chopped
1	large bay leaf
6	c. chicken or veggie stock
1/3	c. sour cream
✍	salt and pepper to taste
☺	minced parsley, sprinkle cardamom

In saucepan, melt butter over low heat. Add cumin, coriander, ginger and cook a few moments. Add carrot and onion. Cover and let cook 8-10 minutes.

Add potatoes, bay leaf and stock. Simmer, covered, until veggies are tender, about 40 minutes. Discard bay leaf.

Puree soup in processor or blender. Return to pot; stir in sour cream and season. Heat gently. Garnish each bowl with parsley and cardamom.

Cream of Mushroom-Asparagus Soup
6 servings

½ lb. mushrooms, separate stems and caps (I wash the mushrooms just before cooking them, to avoid that slimy feeling), slice caps.
1 lb. asparagus
2 Tbs. butter
2 Tbs. olive oil
1 tsp. Spike seasoning salt
1 large onion. chopped
3 cloves garlic, chopped
1 medium carrot, chopped
6 c. vegetable or chicken broth
¼ c. parsley leaves
4 fresh basil leaves
1 tsp. tarragon
½ c. heavy cream
✍ salt, pepper to taste

Peel off woody bottoms of asparagus to tender core. Break off tips and set aside. Chop stems coarsely.

Saute half the sliced mushrooms in hot butter-oil with Spike, in large saucepan until soft, about 6-10 minutes. Remove with slotted spoon and set aside.

Add onions, garlic, carrot, and rest of mushroom caps and stems to oil and saute until tender, about 15 minutes.

Stir in broth and herbs and simmer about 30 minutes. Blend in blender till smooth.

Add asparagus tips and sautéed mushrooms and simmer 10 minutes more. Add cream and heat and serve.

Easy Cream of Potato Soup
6 servings

Cook till tender-mushy, covered:
4 medium potatoes, chopped
2 c. water or bouillon

Right in pot, mash ¾ of potatoes with potato masher and add:
3 c. half & half
3 Tbs. butter

2 Tbs. flour
1/3 c. minced parsley
1-2 tsp. Spike seasoning salt
¼ tsp. pepper

Mix well and simmer till hot and thick.

Cream of Lentil Soup
6-8 servings

1 lb. (2¼ c.) dry lentils, soaked 1 hour, drained
4 c. water
4 c. chicken or vegetable broth or bouillon
3 leeks, trimmed and chopped
3 medium potatoes, chopped
1 large onion, chopped
2 Tbs. butter
2 tsp. ground cumin
1 tsp. ground coriander
✎ salt, pepper
2 c. whipping cream
☺ plain yogurt, as garnish

Add first four ingredients to lentils in large soup pot and bring to boil then turn down and simmer till lentils are tender, 30-60 minutes. Puree in blender till smooth.

While lentils are cooking, saute onions and spices in butter 10 minutes. Add to lentils with salt and pepper, to taste. Continue cooking.

Return pureed lentils to pot and heat with cream. Garnish bowls.

Broccoli Cream Soup
6 servings

8 c. chopped broccoli (1 large bunch)
2 c. stock or water with bouillon
3 Tbs. flour
2 c. half & half
3 Tbs. butter
¼ c. minced parsley
1 tsp. Spike seasoning salt
½ tsp. onion powder
¼ tsp. pepper
☺ pinch rosemary
3 oz. cream cheese

Trim off the woody outside of broccoli stalks and chop all of broccoli.

Simmer broccoli in stock till tender. Blend 2/3 of broccoli in blender with flour and half & half.

Heat butter with parsley and seasonings. Add all broccoli. Heat without boiling and mix in cream cheese till melted and smooth.

Dairyless "Cream" of Tomato Soup
5-6 servings

Grind together in blender:
- 1 c. cashews
- 3 c. water
- 3 Tbs. flour

Heat together in pot 2 minutes:
- 3 Tbs. butter or oil or mix
- 2 tsp. oregano
- 1 tsp. basil
- 1 tsp. dill
- 1 tsp. Spike seasoning salt
- ½ tsp. thyme
- ¼ tsp. pepper

Add and simmer 10 minutes:
- 4 c. chopped fresh tomatoes

Blend ½ of cooked tomatoes with blended cashews and pour all back in pot. Simmer 10-15 minutes.

Add other veggies, if desired

Clam Chowder
6-8 servings

- 1 10 oz. can baby clams and juice
- 1/3 c. minced parsley
- 3 Tbs. butter
- 3 Tbs. flour
- 1 c. whipping cream
- 2 c. diced potatoes
- ½ c. diced carrots
- 3 lg. green onions, chopped
- 2 small zucchini, sliced
- 1 stalk celery, minced
- 3 c. chicken or vegetable stock, or bouillon
- ½ tsp. salt
- ¼ tsp. pepper

Melt butter in saucepan and cook clams with juice and parsley a few minutes. Mix in flour and cook a few minutes. Whisk in cream and cook, stirring, till thickened and bubbly.

Cook potatoes and carrots in stock 10 minutes. Add rest of veggies and cook 8-10 minutes more, till tender.

Pour veggies and stock into clam and cream. Season and serve.

Green Chile Chicken Stew
6-8 servings

Green chile stew, in all it's many variations, is cooked and served throughout New Mexico. Everyone has a favorite version. This is the one we served at "the Ranch", in Taos. It was a daily special that never got old.

3-4 chicken breasts (1 lb.)
1 c. stock or water
✎ pinch pepper and rosemary
5 c. chicken stock or bouillon
2-3 large potatoes, cut in large chunks
1 large carrot, split down middle, cut in 1" chunks
3 Tbs. olive oil
1 large onion, chopped small
1 rib celery, split down middle and chopped small
3 cloves garlic, minced
1 tsp. oregano
1 tsp. Spike seasoning salt
1 tsp. onion powder
1 tsp. thyme
3 Tbs. flour
1-2 Tbs. green chile powder, if you can find it
2-3 c. roasted green chilies, chopped small

Simmer chicken in 1 c. water, with pepper and rosemary over very low heat, till just turned white in middle, about 10-15 minutes.

Cut chicken in large, bite-size cubes and set aside. Add broth to 5 c. stock in large pot. Add potatoes and carrots to stock and cook till tender, about 20 minutes.

While veggies are cooking, heat oil in skillet and saute onions, garlic, celery and herbs, till onions are tender, 10 minutes. Stir in flour and brown 5 minutes.

Mix the onions and herbs in with potatoes and stock and green chilies and powder. Mix well.

Bring to a boil and then simmer 5 minutes. Add chicken and simmer 5 more minutes.

Vegetarian Main Dishes

The Meat and Potatoes of Vegetables

I came from a family where the steady diet was meat, bread and potatoes for breakfast, lunch and dinner. Oh my! One could sink, indeed! And yet, that meat and potatoes has a comforting ring to it, and you might find some of its substantialness in the recipes of this book.

Most of the people I have cooked for this past half of my life have been vegetarians– just like my daughter. And, really, I eat vegetables too!. But personally I like a bit o' meat in my diet, to keep me firmly planted on this particular planet– "grounded" is the word for it. Of course, one doesn't want to get too grounded. It's also good to fly like free little birds with dreams of glory. It's a balancing act, indeed.

So, to be sure, that's what we need– vegetables!– the happy meeting ground! Nourishing! Flavorful! Offering balance and sustenance on which to soar! Presenting for our use an infinite variety of tastes, textures, colors, combinations and creative opportunities!

I have to thank my extended family community for giving me the inspiration to explore the succulent world of vegetables. Without your hungry needs, perhaps I wouldn't have found what is delicious and interesting in so many vegetables, nor have made them so much a part of my life!

Spinach Turnovers - Spanikopita
8-9 large turnovers

Before making these for the Trade Fair, Rita made them. They were the beginning of their popular use here in town. And then came other fillings..

Filling:
Mix all together well:

- 3   10 oz pkg. frozen, chopped spinach, thawed and squeezed mostly dry
- 2   Tbs. fresh lemon juice
- 2   Tbs. basil, minced, fresh
- 2   Tbs. dill, if desired
- 1-2   tsp. onion powder
- ½   tsp. garlic powder
- 1   tsp. grated orange peel
- ½   tsp. pepper
- 1   c. crumbled feta
- 1½   c. cottage cheese or ricotta
- 1   lb. fillo dough, thawed by directions on package
- 1½   c. butter, melted and hot

Assemble the following before opening the fillo, as it dries out quickly and needs to be covered when it is not being worked:

- ♥ hot butter
- ♥ pastry brush, 3" wide is good
- ♥ small knife
- ♥ fillo
- ♥ ½ c. dry measuring cup
- ♥ cookie sheet
- ♥ counter space
- ♥ filling ready to go

Place fillo in front of you, unrolled and positioned with long edge facing you. Put butter above fillo. Cookie sheet goes on one side, filling on other.

Loosen top sheet and without removing it, butter the top horizontal half only, using long, even strokes. (Don't leave brush in butter as it gets drippy-soggy.) Fold the bottom half of sheet up, lengthwise, over the buttered top half. Then butter the bottom half of the sheet underneath it. Fold this one also over the top half. Turn the 2 sheets over as a unit and butter the bottom part. You now have a 4-layer, buttered long, thin rectangle. Fold up the lengthwise, open edges of the fillo to make the width 5", if needed, as different brands have different widths.

Place a rounded ½ c. of filling on bottom corner of one edge. Shape it into a triangle to fill that corner. Fold the lower corner triangle of fillo-filling to meet the top edge, with filling tucked inside. Keeping it tight, fold it along the length, like a flag: up, over, down, over, up, down, folding to the end.

Butter both sides of triangle, place on cookie sheet and make more. Bake at 375° for 20-25 minutes, till golden brown.

Can freeze before baking. Bake 10 minutes longer. Do not thaw before baking.

Stuffed Potatoes
6 big ones

6   big, special Russet "bakers"
½   c. butter
1   tsp. Spike seasoning salt
1   tsp. oregano
1   tsp. marjoram leaves
½   tsp. thyme
½   tsp. rosemary needles
½   tsp. paprika
2   tsp. onion powder
1   tsp. salt
½   tsp. pepper
¾   c. milk
3-4   c. grated favorite cheese
1   c. frozen green peas
☺   paprika for garnish

Oil potatoes; bake at 350° until tender when pierced with fork. Cool until still hot but easy to handle and still soft. Don't wait till they are cold! Slice the tops off and carefully scoop out the innards, scraping skins lightly. (I had a large spoon with a sharp front edge for this job)

Heat butter with spices and herbs. Mash potatoes with butter and milk while potato is still hot. Don't worry about a few lumps- adds interest. Mix in cheese and peas. Fill jackets, sprinkle with paprika and bake at 350° 30-45 minutes, till melty. (Another Trade Fair yummy)

Broccoli Enchilada Casserole
8-9 servings

2   10 oz. cans red enchilada sauce
½   c. salsa
3   c. broccoli, chopped coarse and steamed tender
1   15 oz. can chili beans, with sauce
2   c. cottage cheese
4   c. grated jack cheese or mild cheddar
18   corn tortillas

Heat sauce and salsa in skillet wider than the tortillas. Dip 6 tortillas in sauce and layer in bottom of 9"x12" non-metal baking dish. Spread all of beans over tortillas and sprinkle ½ of cheese. Dip and layer another 6 tortillas. Spoon some extra sauce over them. Spread with broccoli, cottage cheese and rest of cheese.

Dip and top with last 6 tortillas. Spread with remaining sauce. Cover with aluminum foil, puffed up so it doesn't touch the casserole (acid dissolves aluminum), and bake at 350° for 25-30 minutes, until bubbly and melty looking. (Can always stick your finger in the middle to see if it's hot) Let stand at room temp 20 minutes before serving.

Garnish with grated cheese, sour cream and some minced greenery.

Pablano Chilies in Cream
4-6 servings
When roasted, pablanos have a rich, smoky, somewhat hot flavor. They are very Southwest, but have been finding their way north, 'cuz they are so good!

6-8 plump pablanos (green and mild, fat on stem end, tapering to a point), roasted and peeled
2 c. grated jack cheese
¾ c. whipping cream
¾ c. sour cream
✎ parmesan cheese and black pepper, for garnish

Roasting peppers means to place them over or under an open flame and char the outer peel off. I use the flame on my gas stove. Place them right on the burner and turn them as they char black. When charred all over, rinse under a thin stream of cold water. Cut out ends and scrape out seeds. Can also roast them in the broiler.

Pack insides of chilies with cheese. Place in glass baking dish. Mix the two creams together and pour over top. Bake at 350° for 20-25 minutes, till melted. Sprinkle with garnish, and maybe some green.

Serve with something corn.

Enchiladas Verdes
8-10 servings

Blend to a paste in blender or food processor:
5 pablano chilies
1 c. green tomatillos (blanch in boiling water 1 minute and peel shell, or use
2 eggs

Fold in and set aside:
½ c. minced cilantro
3 green onions, minced
1 c. broken black olives

Heat in skillet:
2 Tbs. oil
1 Tbs. chili powder
1 tsp. onion powder
½ tsp. garlic powder

Add and mash well:
1 28 oz. can chili beans

Heat in a touch of oil- just enuf to make them foldable:
1 dozen tortillas

Fill tortillas with beans and
¼ c. grated cheese, each (3 c.)

Fold in half and arrange in greased 9"x12" non-metal baking dish. Pour green sauce evenly over top Bake at 350°, uncovered, 25-30 minutes, until set.

Garnish with:
1 c. sour cream

Spinach Lasagna
9-12 servings
This is a "miniaturized" version of the lasagna I served every Saturday at the Trade Fair for many years running

Sauce:
- 2 29 oz. cans tomato sauce
- 1 12 oz. can tomato paste
- 1 c. water
- ½ c. olive oil
- 3 Tbs. oregano
- 3 Tbs. basil
- 1 Tbs. marjoram
- 1 tsp. thyme
- 2 tsp. onion powder
- 1 tsp. garlic powder
- ½ tsp. pepper

Heat oil at low temp (too hot will burn the herbs) and cook herbs a few minutes, to unleash flavor.
Add tomato sauce, paste, water (rinse out cans with it) and simmer ½ hour, uncovered.

Fillings:
- 12 lasagna noodles, uncooked
- 1 10 oz. pkg. frozen chopped spinach, thawed, juicy

- 2 c. ricotta or cottage cheese
- 1 c. Parmesan cheese
- 3 c. grated mozzarella or jack cheese

Using a deep 9"x12" or 10"x14" baking pan, assemble layers in following order, spreading:
- 2 c. sauce
- 4 noodles
- ☺ half each of spinach, cottage cheese, cheese
- ¼ c. Parmesan
- 3 c. sauce
- 4 noodles (push down gently to level the ingredients)
- ☺ other half of spinach, cottage cheese and cheese
- ¼ c. Parmesan
- 2 c. sauce
- 4 noodles (level it all again)
- ☺ rest of sauce
- ½ c. Parmesan, evenly over top

Bake at 350° for 45-60 minutes, covered. If using aluminum foil, tent so it doesn't touch sauce, as you would be eating metal.

Let set 20 minutes before cutting.

White Lasagna with Artichoke Hearts
8 servings

2   Tbs. oil or butter
1   medium onion, chopped
4   cloves garlic, minced
2   c. vegetable broth
1   tsp. rosemary leaves
½   tsp. sage leaves
1   14 oz. can artichoke hearts
1   10 oz. pkg. frozen, chopped
    spinach, thawed and juicy
4   c. cream sauce, from any
    source (even "store
    bought")
1   c. ricotta, mixed with
¼   tsp. pepper
10 lasagna noodles, uncooked
3   c. grated mozzarella (12 oz)
1   c. feta cheese, crumbled

Heat oil and cook onions and garlic several minutes. Stir in herbs and broth. Heat to boiling and add artichoke hearts and spinach. Cover and simmer a few minutes. Stir in cream sauce.

Spread 2 c. sauce in bottom of 12"x9" baking pan. Layer with 4 lasagna noodles. Top with ½ of ricotta and 1 c. mozzarella and 1/3 of rest of sauce. Layer once more with 3 noodles topping with third of sauce and 1 c. cheese. Layer with 3 noodles and last of sauce and cheese. Sprinkle with feta cheese.

Cover and bake 45 minutes at 350°. Bake uncovered 10 minutes. Let stand 15 minutes before cutting.

Broccoli Dijon
12 squares

1   pkg. fillo leaves, thawed
½-¾   c. butter, melted, hot
1   large bunch broccoli, peel
      woody stems, chop bite-
      size, steam lightly
2   tsp. Dijon mustard
2   c. cottage cheese or ricotta
2½   c. grated tangy cheese, like
      sharp cheddar or gruyere
1/3   c. Parmesan
1   tsp. dill weed
♥   salt, pepper

Butter glass baking dish, 10"x15" Loosen top fillo sheet and butter it. Place in dish, up the sides a bit. Repeat, using half of the sheets. Spread mustard evenly over bottom crust, followed by broccoli, cheeses, dill, salt and pepper. Top with remaining sheets, buttering, and tuck edges under. Score top sheets into 3x4 rows. Bake at 375° 25 minutes, till brown. Cut thru and serve.

Eggplant Parmesan
8 servings

Sauce:
- 4 Tbs. olive oil
- 1 32 oz. can tomatoes, undrained, cut up
- 1 6 oz. can tomato paste
- 1 Tbs. oregano
- 1 Tbs. basil
- ¼ tsp. pepper
- 1 tsp. onion powder
- ½ tsp. garlic powder

Heat oil, add spices, then tomatoes. Simmer 30 minutes.

- 1 large eggplant, unpeeled, cut in ½" slices
- 2 eggs, beaten with 1 Tbs. water
- ½ c. bread crumbs
- ½ c. Parmesan cheese
- ☺ more olive oil

Mix together crumbs and Parmesan. Dip eggplant slices in egg, then the crumb mix.

Fry in hot oil until golden brown, adding a thin layer of oil as needed. Don't put eggplant in cold oil. Soaks it up like a sponge.

Drain on paper towels. Or try the baking method: Place crumb coated pieces on well oiled baking sheet. Drizzle olive oil over tops. Bake at 400° 10-12 minutes, until golden brown on bottom sides of eggplant. Turn and bake 10-12 minutes to brown other side.

Topping:
- ½ lb. mozzarella, sliced thin
- 2/3 c. Parmesan

Spread 1/3 of tomato sauce in bottom of 9"x 12" non-metal baking pan. Arrange ½ of eggplant over sauce. Top with cheese and ½ of parmesan. Spread with 1/3 more sauce.

Layer rest of eggplant and mozzarella. Spread with last of sauce and sprinkle with last of parmesan.

Bake at 350° for 25 minutes. Let rest 15 minutes before cutting.

California Casserole
6-8 servings

To California Dressing recipe add:
- 2 c. cooked beans (16 oz. can)
- 2 c. grated cheese
- 1 c. broth or bouillon

Mix well and place in a well-buttered casserole. Cover and bake at 350° for 45 minutes, till hot.

Baked Fondue
8-10 servings

Thick, custardy and savory. Prepare the day before.

1½ long loaves French bread, cut ½" thick
½ c. soft butter
½ c. nice mustard, like Green Peppercorn mustard
3 c. grated or sliced cheese, like sharp cheddar
4 eggs, well beaten
5 c. milk, hot
1½ tsp. Worcestershire sauce
½ tsp. salt
¼ tsp. pepper, or more

Blend together mustard and butter and spread on bread. Combine milk, eggs and seasonings.

Alternate layers of bread and cheese in buttered 4 qt. baking dish. Pour milk over all and sprinkle with paprika. Cover and refrigerate till next day.

Bake at 350° for 90 minutes or more, depending on how thick it is layered.

Cauliflower Nut-Crumb
6-8 servings
This is a great family favorite. The topping is good for other dishes.

Steam till crisp-tender:
1 head cauliflower, cut in flowerets

Mix and add to cauliflower:
2 c. grated cheddar cheese
1 c. sour cream or cottage cheese
½ c. milk
½ tsp. Dijon mustard
Spread in buttered casserole dish:

Nut-Crumb Topping:
Cook in pan a few minutes:
1/3 c. melted butter
1 tsp. Spike seasoning salt
1 c. chopped walnuts
½ c. bread crumbs
½ c. Parmesan cheese
¼ tsp. pepper

Spread over cauliflower. Bake 20 minutes at 350°, till melty and hot.

Manicotti
Makes 14 shells

1 box manicotti, cooked al dente, rinsed

Tomato sauce:
1 29 oz. can tomato sauce
1/3 c. olive oil
1 Tbs. basil
2 tsp. marjoram
2 tsp. oregano

Heat oil and herbs together a minute and add tomato sauce.

Simmer, stirring occasionally, uncovered, about 30 minutes.

Fillings: Mix together well:
2½ lbs. ricotta (5 cups)and 3 eggs, or 2 c. ricotta and 1 lb. grated mozzarella or Gouda, or 3 c. ricotta and 2 c. grated cheese
½ c. Parmesan

3-4 green onions, minced
4 Tbs. minced parsley
1 c. chopped green or black olives, if desired
✍ salt, pepper to taste

To assemble manicotti, carefully fill each tube, a generous 1/3 c. each, by squeezing mixture into sausage shape and poking in. Spread half tomato sauce on bottom of 9"x12" non-metal baking pan. Arrange tubes on sauce and pour rest over top.

Bake, uncovered for firmer texture, and covered for juicier, softer results, until hot and melted, at 350°, 30-40 minutes.

Substitute giant shells for manicotti. Bake either pasta in cream sauce rather than red sauce, for a change.

Fideos Secos
4-5 servings
Given to me by Edith, a roommate in college, made by her Spanish mother

3 twists fine vermicelli, either whole wheat or white
1 onion, minced
1/3 c. oil
2 tomatoes, chopped small
2 c. vegetable or chicken broth
2 tsp. your choice of basil, oregano, thyme or oregano
1 c. grated cheese
✍ salt, pepper to taste

Brown vermicelli in oil, both sides. Remove from pan, with all the little bits. Cook onion in pan next, till soft. Add rest of ingredients, mix and bring to boil.

Add vermicelli, cover, and simmer till dry. In the last few minutes, sprinkle on cheese and cover till melted.

Potato-Cheese Turnovers
6-8 large turnovers

¾	lb. fillo dough, thawed
7	c. potatoes, cut in ½" cubes
½	c. minced green onions
¼	c. minced parsley
¼	c. minced green pepper
3	Tbs. butter
2	tsp. Spike seasoning salt
¼	tsp. pepper
3	c. grated mild cheese, like Jack or Havarti

Cook potatoes in water till tender. Drain. In skillet, melt butter. Add seasonings and greens and cook a few minutes. Add potatoes and mix well. Cool. Mix in cheese.

Make turnovers as described in Spinach Turnovers.

Pizza
Two 12" rounds, 8 pieces each

Sauce: Saute in 1/3 c. olive oil:

½	c. chopped green pepper
½	c. minced parsley
1	Tbs. basil
1	Tbs. oregano
1	tsp. marjoram
1	tsp. onion powder
½	tsp. garlic powder
½	tsp. thyme
1	bay leaf

Add and simmer, covered, for 2 hours:

20	oz. can tomato sauce
6	oz. tomato paste
1	c. water

Dough: Dissolve together:

2	pkg. dry baking yeast
1¼	c. warm-hot water

Add to yeast and mix to a dough:

3½	c. flour
2	Tbs. oil
1	tsp. salt

Knead till smooth and elastic. Roll around in oiled bowl, cover, let rise till doubled. Divide in half. Form each half into a flat round and let set 10-15 minutes, or longer. Roll, push and stretch into two 12" rounds and placed on well oiled round baking pans. (Can use cookie sheets instead of rounds.)

Spread with tomato sauce and any of the following:
- black and/or green olives
- sliced green pepper, onion, tomato, zucchini, or other
- turkey sausage or ham
- etc.,etc.

And don't forget:
3-4c. grated cheese
☺ lots of Parmesan

Bake at 400° for 15-20 minutes, on bottom shelf, close to heat.

Carol's Spectacular Gourmet Different Pizza
With dried tomatoes! The vegetarians' answer to anchovies.

Start with pizza crust as usual but here's where it changes:

Soak ½ c. per pizza of dried tomatoes, in boiling water poured over, till soft. Or you can use the dried tomatoes packed in olive oil and bypass soak step. Cut tomatoes in squares. Brush cookie sheet and prepared crust generously on top with olive oil

Sprinkle on top in order written:
- ☺ prepared dried tomatoes
- ½ c. each pizza, sliced green olives
- ☺ fresh or dried oregano, basil, tarragon
- 2 c. per pizza jalapeno jack grated cheese
- ☺ sprinkle Parmesan lavishly
- ☺ sprinkle olive oil lavishly

Bake as regular pizza.

Spinach-Stuffed Pizza Boats
10 generous pieces
This was a putting together of many leftovers and was so tasty it became a repeat, i.e., recipe

1 long fresh French bread, sliced in half lengthwise, horizontally to make 2 long, flat logs
½ c. soft butter
2 10 oz. pkg. frozen chopped spinach, defrosted
2 c. cottage cheese, ricotta, cream sauce or cheese sauce
½ c. Parmesan
1 tsp. Spike seasoning salt
🖐 pepper to taste
3-4 c. prepared thick pizza sauce
4 c. grated cheese
🖐 Parmesan cheese
🖐 "fruity" olive oil

Mix squeezed spinach with ricotta, cottage cheese, or cream sauce, ½ c. parmesan, Spike and pepper.

Spread butter generously over crust of bread lengths. Place buttered halves on cookie sheet, side-by-side, soft side up. Spread with tomato sauce. Carefully spoon on spinach filling.

Top with grated cheese and sprinkle on parmesan and olive oil. Bake at 350° for 20 minutes till melted and hot thruout, with a crispy crust.

Slice 5-6 pieces per boat.

Peas and Panir
4-6 servings

Panir (prepared a day earlier)
2 qts. milk
ễ juice of at least 2 lemons

Heat milk over medium heat in heavy pot to just under boiling, when there are lots of bubbles. (Be sure to keep it from scorching as it ruins the flavor.) Stir in most of the lemon juice and watch the curd and whey separate. If whey is not clear, add more lemon juice and stir. Whey should be clear. Pour into a colander lined with cheese cloth or other thin, porous fabric. Reserve ¾ c. of whey.

When top of curds are dry-10-15 minutes- use a spatula to scrap it all together and smooth top. Let drain 8-12 hours in fridge. Cut in 1" cubes.

Peas
6 Tbs. ghee or butter
2 tsp. black mustard seed
1 c. chopped onion
2 cloves garlic, minced
¾ c. reserved whey
4 Tbs. grated fresh ginger
1½ Tbs. garam masala
3 tsp. ground coriander
2 tsp. ground cumin
1½ tsp. turmeric
🖅 shake of red pepper flakes
1 tsp. salt, or more
½ c. minced fresh cilantro
4 c. chopped tomatoes
3 c. green peas, fresh or frozen

Fry panir in 4 Tbs. of the ghee. Carefully turn and brown all sides. Remove to a dish.

Add remaining ghee and mustard seed and cook till they start popping. Stir in ginger, onions and garlic. Saute and stir 3-5 minutes.

Have rest of spices mixed together in a small bowl. Stir in spices and whey and mix and cook for 5 minutes.

Add tomatoes, cover and bring to a boil. Then turn down and simmer, stirring occasionally, for 15-20 minutes. Stir in peas and 6 Tbs. of cilantro, simmer 10 minutes. Stir in panir towards end and cook just long enuf to heat panir. Serve with rice. Garnish with rest of cilantro.

Garam Masala

Mix all together and store in airtight jar:
1 Tbs. ground cumin
1 Tbs. cinnamon
2 tsp. black pepper
1 tsp. cloves
1 tsp. ground cardamom

Traditionally, one gets these spices whole, shells the cardamom, and grinds it all together. This recipe is streamlined for busy people who still want a touch of "from scratch."

Deep-Dish Pizza Pie
8-10 wedges

1 pie crust recipe (2 crusts)

Sauce: Cook together a few minutes:
- 1/3 c. olive oil
- 1 Tbs. oregano
- 1 Tbs. basil
- 1 tsp. marjoram

Add to sauce and simmer 5 minutes:
- 8 oz. can tomato sauce
- 12 oz. tomato puree
- 2 c. broken black olives

Filling: Mix together in a bowl:
- 1 lb. ricotta
- 1 c. Parmesan
- 4 Tbs. minced chives or green onion
- 2 Tbs. minced parsley
- 4 eggs (or ¼ c. flour)
- ½ tsp. pepper

Fix to stand by:
- 2 c. grated mozzarella
- 1 small zucchini, thin sliced and lightly steamed
- ½ green pepper, sliced thin

Line 9" deep dish pie plate with bottom pastry. Spread with half of ricotta mix. Spread with half mozzarella and veggies and cover with half of sauce. Repeat with remaining halves. Cover with top crust and crimp. (See instructions in Basic Pie Crust recipe.)

Bake at 375° for 35 minutes.

Let set for 20 minutes before serving.

Basic Quiche
8 small pieces

- ½ recipe pie crust, unbaked, lining a 9" pie plate
- 3 eggs
- 2 c. milk, half & half, or even whipping cream
- ½ tsp. onion powder
- ¼ tsp. salt
- pinch nutmeg
- pinch pepper
- paprika, tomato slices, for garnish

Beat eggs slightly and whisk in rest to smoothness.

Arrange on bottom of pie crust:
- 1 c. cubed cheese of choice, such as Gruyere, Gouda, Swiss or Cheddar

Try with the cheese:
- ½ c. cooked, cup up fake bacon, or
- ½ thick sliced potato, cooked

Pour filling over cheese. Sprinkle paprika over top or arrange tomato slices. Bake at 350° for 40-45 minutes

Tofu Quiche
8 servings

½ pie crust recipe
4 generous cups of chopped broccoli or zucchini, or mix
2-3 Tbs. butter
2 tsp. Spike seasoning salt
1 tsp. paprika
½ tsp. rosemary
¼ tsp. cumin
☺ pinch thyme
✐ pepper, to taste

Saute spices in butter a few moments, add veggies, mixing well. Cover and cook on low a few minutes.

Mix well together:
1 lb. tofu, mashed
1 c. cottage cheese
1/3 c. Parmesan
1 Tbs. prepared mustard
1/3 c. flour or 2 eggs
2 c. grated cheese

Add sautéd veggies to tofu mix. Turn into prepared pie crust in 9" deep dish pie plate. Bake at 350° for 40 minutes.

Vegetable "Pot" Pie
8 servings

1 pie crust recipe
1 small potato, cubed ½"
1 small carrot, cubed
2 c. broccoli, cauliflower or zucchini, cubed
1 c. water
1 bouillon cube
1½ c. half & half
3 eggs
2 tsp. Spike
¼ tsp. pepper
1 c. peas
2 c. cubed cheese, your choice

Simmer potato and carrot in water with bouillon for 10 minutes, till tender. Remove with slotted spoon and add remaining veggies and cook them 5 minutes, till almost tender. Drain veggies and drink juice!

Beat milk, eggs and seasonings together and add veggies, peas and cheese.

Pour into prepared crust in deep dish 9" pie plate, and cover with second crust, crimping.

Bake at 350° for 25-35 minutes, till brown.

Vegetable-Noodle Pie
8 pieces

1 pie crust recipe
Make a cream sauce with:(See
Cheese Sauce recipe for
procedure)
- ¼ c. butter
- ¼ c. flour
- 2 tsp. Spike seasoning salt
- 1 tsp. tarragon leaf
- ½ tsp. paprika
- ¼ tsp. pepper
- 2 c. milk
- 1½ c. your favorite noodle
(broad egg noodles are good
unless you want to sink
your teeth into something
more hefty, like mosticelli,
or those snailish things)

- 3 c. chopped mixed veggies-
like zucchini, cauliflower,
carrot, parsnip, green bean
- ½ c. green peas

Mix together cream sauce, noodles
and veggies. Cool.

Line 9" deep dish pie plate with
bottom crust. Fill and cover with
top crust. (See Pie Crust recipe)

Bake at 375° for 10 minutes and
350° for 20-25 minutes, until
golden brown. Let set 15 minutes
before cutting.

Spinach Pie or Croustade
8 pieces

1 pie crust recipe
- 4 Tbs. butter
- 1/3 c. flour
- 2 tsp. Spike seasoning salt
- 1 tsp. tarragon
- ¼ tsp. pepper
- 2 c. milk
- 1 16 oz bag frozen, chopped
spinach, thawed, squeezed,
or 2 bunch fresh, prepped,
chopped and steamed very
lightly (about 3 cups)
- 3 eggs

Make cream sauce (see Cheese
Sauce recipe) with butter, flour,
seasonings and milk. Cool and beat
in eggs. Fold in spinach.
Fill pastry-lined 9" pie plate with
spinach, cover with top crust and
crimp. Bake at 350° for 30 min.

Croustade Version: (see Spinach
Turnover recipe for technique.)
Use:
- 10 sheets fillo, thawed
- ½ c. butter, melted

Butter each sheet and fold it in
thirds, brushing top. Arrange
them in 9" pie plate by overlapping
in center and hanging off pie plate
like spokes on a wheel. Pile on the
spinach. Starting with the last
spoke, lift it up towards the
center, twisting and tucking under
to form a rosette. Lay it over
filling, leaving a 3" circle in
center. Do with all. Drizzle on
leftover butter. Bake at 375° for
35-40 minutes, until golden.
Really impressive!

Southwest Egg Bake
6-8 servings

1   15 oz. can black beans, drained
2   Tbs. vegetable oil
½   onion, chopped fine
½   c. chopped green pepper
4   cloves garlic, minced
2   c. corn kernels
1   c. chopped, roasted green chile (if frozen, defrost and drain just a little)
4   c. frozen shredded potatoes (hash browns)
2-3 c. grated jack cheese
8   eggs
2   c. milk
½   tsp. salt
✍   Spike seasoning salt
1   tomato, chopped small
3   green onions, sliced

Butter well a 9"x12" non-metal baking dish. Spread black beans evenly over bottom.

Saute onions, green pepper and garlic in oil several minutes. Fold onion mix into corn, green chile, potatoes and cheese. Spread evenly on beans.

Whisk together eggs, milk and salt. Pour carefully over veggies in baking dish. Sprinkle with Spike. Bake at 350° for 55 minutes, until set in middle.

Garnish with tomato and green onion.

Zucchini Bake with Mushrooms and Ricotta
4 servings

4   zucchini, ¼" slices
½   lb. mushrooms, sliced
½   c. onion, chopped
2   Tbs. butter
1   tsp. Spike seasoning salt
½   tsp. basil
½   tsp. oregano
✍   pinch nutmeg
✍   pepper, to taste
1   c. ricotta
½   lb. havarti cheese, grated
2   Tbs. parmesan
1   c. tomato sauce (8 oz.)
✍   Parmesan, garnish

Steam zucchini tender. In skillet, melt butter and cook mushrooms and onion with Spike and seasonings till onions are softened, 5 minutes.

Cover buttered bottom of 2 quart casserole with half the zucchini. Top with mushroom mix. Spread on ricotta, sprinkle on parmesan and half the cheese. Add rest of zucchini. Cover with tomato sauce. Sprinkle with rest of cheese and more parmesan.

Bake at 350° for 25 minutes.

Goulash with Eggplant
4-6 servings

1   recipe Fresh Tomato Sauce
2   Tbs. olive oil
1   small eggplant, cut in 1" cubes, about 2 c.
3   medium zucchini, halved lengthwise and sliced thin
½   c. each, sliced green olives and green onion
4   oz. can chopped green chile
16   oz. can garbanzo beans

Saute eggplant in hot oil 5 minutes. Add zucchini and cook 5 more minutes. Add rest and simmer 15 minutes, stirring occasionally.

Add to goulash and stir till heated and melted:

1   c. small elbow pasta, cooked
1   c. sharp cheddar or feta
4   oz. cream cheese, cubed

Eggplant Pockets
12 pockets

1   large eggplant, sliced at an angle in ¼" thick pieces, making big, flat slabs.
3-4   c. Fresh Tomato Sauce, or other sauce of your choice
½   lb. Mozzarella, or other favorite cheese, like Swiss or Fontina, cut into slabs ¼" thick by 1" x 2"-3"

Try other interesting tid-bits to wrap in pocket as a surprise, such as chopped olive, crumb mixes (Nut-Crumb Mix, Almond-Crumb Mix), peppercorns, dried tomato, artichoke, ricotta, green onion, or toasted pine nuts.
♥   olive oil, for frying
♥   Parmesan cheese

Prepare tomato sauce as directed

Eggplants are oil guzzlers, so use only a teaspoon or so of oil at a time to fry the eggplant, frying a few slices at a time. Fry a few minutes each side, to soften them enough to be rolled up. Repeat and set aside, frying smaller end pieces also.

Place 1 c. of sauce in 9"x12" non-metal baking dish. Place a cheese slice in the middle of the eggplant slab, with any other goodies. Fold both ends over the filling and set in sauce in dish.

Put smaller pieces of eggplant together to make a larger one to fill. Cover all with sauce and Parmesan. Bake at 350° for 20-30 minutes, until hot and melted.

Fettuccini Alfredo with Vegetables
6-8 servings

12 oz. fettuccini noodles, cooked by package directions
3 c. steamed, cut broccoli
1 c. steamed snow peas, crisp but hot
15 oz. can baby corn, halved lengthwise

Sauce:
2/3 c. butter
1 tsp. crushed sage leaf
1 tsp. dry basil or 1-2 Tbs. fresh, minced
1¼ c. Parmesan cheese, try grating fresh.

Start water for noodles. Prep veggies and, while noodles are cooking and veggies steaming (10 minutes for broccoli- add peas and corn last 5 minutes) start sauce.

Melt butter and cook herbs a minute. Add cream and heat to tiny bubble stage. Whisk the Parmesan bit-by-bit. When all is incorporated, sauce should be nice and hot. Place hot, drained noodles on serving platter.

Arrange veggies over noodles and pour sauce over all.

Curried Mixed Vegetable Turnovers
6-7 large ones

1 lb. fillo, thawed
2/3 c. butter, melted
2 c. potatoes, ½" cubes
1½ c. carrots, ½" cubes
2 c. cauliflower, chopped medium fine
1 c. peas or chopped zucchini
3 Tbs. butter
2 tsp. black mustard seed
2 Tbs. grated fresh ginger, or 2 tsp. powdered
1 Tbs. cumin
1 Tbs. ground coriander
1 tsp. turmeric
½ tsp. fenugreek
☺ cayenne, if desired
🖎 salt, pepper to taste

Steam potatoes and carrots till almost tender.

Heat butter in skillet, add mustard seed, and when it pops, add ginger and stir. Add rest of spices and ½ c. water. Cover and steam a few minutes and mix again. Cook another 5-8 minutes, till cauliflower is tender. Mix in potatoes, carrots and peas.

Can be served as a vegetable at this point, with a little more heating. Or, cool completely to make turnovers.

To make large turnovers, see Spinach Turnovers, for medium, see Potato-Spinach Turnovers, and for small, see Curried Chicken Turnovers.

Potato-Spinach Turnovers
12 medium turnovers

5	c. potatoes, cut in ½" bite-size pieces
2	Tbs. oil
2	10 oz. pkg. frozen chopped spinach, thawed, drained
3	Tbs. butter
1	tsp. black mustard seed
2-3	Tbs. grated fresh ginger
2	tsp. cumin
2	tsp. coriander
1	tsp. onion powder
½	tsp. garlic powder
½	tsp. turmeric
¼	tsp. cinnamon
¼	tsp. nutmeg
¼	tsp. clove
1½	tsp. salt
½	tsp. pepper
✎	pinch red pepper
½	c. sour cream, or plain yogurt
1	lb. fillo, thawed
2/3	c. butter, melted and hot

Heat oil in heavy skillet and brown potatoes, all sides. Set aside. Heat butter in pan and add mustard seeds. When they start to sputter, stir in ginger, cook a few minutes, add rest of spices. Stir in spinach, potatoes and sour cream. Cool completely.

To assemble, loosen top sheet of fillo. Brush with butter and fold in thirds. Starting at one corner, place 1/3 c. of filling, shaping as triangle on corner. Fold up as a flag. (see Spinach Turnovers). Brush both sides with butter and place on baking sheet. Bake at 375° for 15-20 minutes, till golden brown. Can be made ahead of time and stored in fridge, but don't freeze any with potatoes in them. Frozen potatoes sog.

Spinach Loaf
8-10 slices

2	10 oz. pkg. frozen, chopped spinach, thawed and drained
24	oz. small curd cottage cheese
½	c. Parmesan cheese
¾	c. bread crumbs, toasted
6	eggs, beaten
1	tsp. Spike seasoning salt
¼	tsp. pepper
½	pkg. instant onion soup mix
¼	c. Parmesan cheese, garnish

Blend all but garnish together well. Adjust salt, pepper.

Line large loaf pan with parchment paper or tin foil and butter well.

Spoon mix into pan and press down. Sprinkle top with Parmesan. Bake at 350° for 30 minutes, until set. Cut in slices. Good hot or cold. Serve with sour cream.

Tofu Stroganoff
Serves 6-8

Here is the long awaited ancient secret recipe from the trade fair days. Somehow it never made it into the stewpot, even though it was sitting there ready to go. But it's faithfully stayed with me all these years, waiting for a chance….

2 lb. tofu, cut in thin, 1" strips
3 Tbs. butter
3 Tbs. oil
3-4 Tbs. Mexican blend seasoning or deluxe chili powder
1 c. water or stock
$\frac{1}{4}$ c. soy sauce or tamari
2 Tbs. flour
4 Tbs. tomato puree
1 tsp. Worcestershire sauce
1 lb. zucchini, sliced thin' and lightly steamed
$1\frac{1}{2}$ c. sour cream
8 oz. your favorite pasta, cooked

Heat butter and oil in heavy skillet and add the tofu strips. As they fry merrily on high, sprinkle the chili powder over them. Let the tofu bottoms brown before turning the tofu and mixing in the chili powder. Fry till chewy looking, well coated with spice and golden brown. Remove from pan and set aside.

Make a paste of water, soy sauce, flour, tomato puree, and Worcestershire sauce. Stir into skillet (just vacated by tofu) with zucchinis and bring to boil, stirring till thickened. Reduce heat and simmer 5 minutes.

Mix in tofu and sour cream and heat gently, just till hot. Do not boil, as it curdles. Serve mixed in or over cooked pasta

Spinach Stuffed Tomatoes
Serves 6

6   ripe, firm, medium
     tomatoes
¼   c. olive oil
5   green onions,
     chopped
1   large bunch spinach,
     chopped, or
10 ounce package frozen
     chopped spinach,
     thawed and drained
¼   c. chopped parsley
¼   c. chopped fresh basil or
     dill or 1 Tbs. dry of either
🖉   pepper to taste
½   c. crumbled feta
     cheese
🖉   parmesan, grated

Slice ½ inch off the top of each tomato and scoop out the innards. Chop pulp and set aside.

In large skillet, sauté onion in hot oil till tender. Add tomato pulp, spinach, and seasonings and cook over high heat until most of the liquid is absorbed- 5 minutes. Stir in feta cheese. Cool.

Fill tomatoes with spinach mix; place in oiled baking dish, sprinkle parmesan on top, and bake at 375° about 20 minutes.

Navajo Tacos
The Southwest has it's special treats, and this is one of them. Greasy but good. It's easy to use in lots of different ways.

1   recipe Indian Fry Bread
1   lb. pintos, soaked overnight
1   lg. onion, chopped
1   tsp. garlic powder
🖉   salt, pepper to taste

Fill with:
🖉   shredded lettuce
🖉   cubed tomatoes
🖉   fine chopped onion
🖉   lots of grated cheese
🖉   olives, salsa, sour cream,
🖉   avocado
🖉   what ever else you might
     think of- maybe tofu, squished
     or cubed and fried to brown-
     ness with a little chile powder

To cook beans:
Drain and cover with water or stock. Add onion and garlic powder and simmer an hour or more, till tender, and water has cooked down. Season to taste. If you need more water during cooking time add only boiling water. Cold water will toughen the bean skins. Semi-mash before placing on taco.

I wonder how Greek would go with fry bread. Sounds good to me!

Corn Casserole
4 servings

2 c. corn kernels (about 5 ears), fresh is good
¾ c. butter, melted
2 eggs
½ c. sour cream
1 c. grated Jack cheese (try jalapeno Jack)
½ c. corn meal
1 4 oz. can chopped green chilies
1 tsp. salt

(handwritten: ½ c. cottage cheese)

Puree corn with butter and eggs in blender.

Mix rest of ingredients in a separate bowl and blend in corn mix.

Bake in greased 2-quart baking dish at 350°, uncovered, for 50-60 minutes.

Try ½ sour cream and ½ cream cheese, cubed small.

Braised White Beans with Wine
4-6 servings

2 c. dried white kidney beans or cannellini beans
10 c. vegetable stock or bouillon
3 lg. bay leaves
2 Tbs. olive oil
1 large onion, julienned
3 cloves garlic, chopped
½ c. red wine
1 c. white wine
3 tomatoes, diced
1 Tbs. chopped fresh rosemary, or 1 tsp. dry
2 tsp. fresh thyme, or ½ tsp. dry
salt, pepper to taste

Soak beans overnight in water. Drain and place in stockpot with stock and bay leaf. Bring to boil, turn down and simmer till done- 2 hours for kidney and ½ hour for cannelllini. Should have about 2 cups of stock left.

In skillet, heat oil and add onions and garlic and fry a few minutes. Add wines and boil until about ½ cup remains. Add beans and tomatoes to onions and bring to boil. Add herbs and cook about 5 minutes. Season and serve.

Very tasty. Can top with a tangy, soft cheese, such as goat or other feta for extra protein and flavor.

Nut Loaf
6-8 servings

Cook, uncovered, 20 minutes, low heat, until tender:
- ½ c. millet
- 2 c. water

Saute in 2 Tbs. oil a few minutes:
- 1 small rib celery, chopped
- ½ c. minced parsley
- ¼ c. grated green pepper
- 1 tsp. Spike seasoning salt
- 1 tsp. oregano
- 1 tsp. rubbed sage
- ✐ pinch rosemary

Mix together well with millet and veggies:
- 1 Tbs. soy sauce or Tamari
- 2½ c. ground nuts, your choice
- 1/3 c. sesame butter or other nut butter
- 1 egg, if desired

Shape into loaf on baking sheet and spread all over with:
- ½ c. catsup

Bake 1 hour at 350°

Filled Pockets
8 pita halves

Filling:
- 2 avocados. mashed
- 1 c. shredded lettuce
- 1 c. chopped tomatoes
- 1 c. chopped cucumbers
- ½ c. sliced green olives
- ✐ few slices green pepper
- ✐ pickled jalapeno slices
- 1 c. grated cheese, if like

4 pita rounds, halved

Toss veggies with a mix of:
- ¼ c. mayo or plain yogurt
- 3 Tbs. fresh lemon juice
- ✐ garlic powder, if desired

Fill pita pockets and serve.
Try fried chick pea balls or cooked shredded chicken.

Easy Baked Beans
6-8 servings

Mix all together:
- 3 15 oz. cans baked beans of your choice
- ½ c. packed brown sugar
- ½ c. catsup
- 2 Tbs. molasses
- 1 Tbs. soy sauce
- 1 Tbs. apple cider vinegar
- 2 tsp. balsamic vinegar
- 2 tsp. prepared mustard
- 1 tsp. powdered ginger
- 1 tsp. onion powder
- ✐ pepper, to taste
- ✐ dashes Worcestershire sauce, if desired

Bake uncovered in a casserole dish at 350° for an hour.

Middle East Savory Lentils
4-6 servings

1 full cup lentils
5-6 c. water
3 Tbs. olive oil
2-3 Tbs. grated fresh ginger
¼ c. grated onion
2 cloves garlic, minced, or
   ½ tsp. garlic powder
2 tsp. ground cumin
2 tsp. ground coriander
½ tsp. fenugreek
½ tsp. turmeric
1 tsp. garam masala or pumpkin
   pie spice
1 tsp. salt
* pinch fennel seed
* pinch cardamom

Cover and simmer lentils in water

1 hour. Uncover and, at low heat, cook down to a paste, stirring occasionally, 1½-2 hours, adding onion at end of cooking time.

Heat oil in small skillet and add garlic, ginger and spices, mixed with a little water, and cook several minutes. Stir into lentils and mix till well blended.

At this point lentils can be served with rice and yogurt and be good. Or try wrapping cooled lentils in large wonton wraps, envelope style, and deep-fry in oil. Try with dip of plain yogurt and roasted cumin seed.

Stuffed Grape Leaves-Dolmathes
3 dozen

Saute in oil till tender:
½ c. olive oil
1 tomato, chopped fine
1 c. grated carrot
1 c. grated zucchini
½ c. minced celery
½ c. minced parsley
1 Tbs. dill weed

Add:
¼ c. fresh lemon juice
1 c. long grain rice, uncooked
½ c. pine nuts
1½ c. broth or bouillon
Bring to a boil, cover, turn down and simmer 20 minutes. Cool.

Rinse and drain:
1 jar (1 lb.) grape leaves

Fill leaves by placing 1 heaping tablespoon of stuffing at stem end of leaf. Roll once, tuck the 2 sides into center over filling and finish rolling up.

Place close together in grape-leaf lined large skillet. Cover with:
   2 c. chicken or veggie broth
   ¼ c. lemon juice
   2 Tbs. olive oil
Place a plate on top to weigh them down. Cover and simmer, lowest heat, ½ hour. Serve warm or cold.

If desired, fry in a little olive oil in skillet, turning to brown all sides, before serving.

Bean Thread (or Rice) Stir Fry
6-8 servings

Soak in hot water for 10 minutes and snip into shorter lengths.

7   oz. rice noodles (trans-
    parent noodles made from
    rice or mung bean)

Prepare:
 3   Tbs. oil
12   oz. pkg. firm tofu, cut in
     strips
 4   green onions, sliced on
     diagonal
 3   c. mixed veggies, such as
     green beans, spinach,
     Chinese cabbage, green
     pepper, snow peas, baby
     corn, mushrooms, broccoli,
     sliced diagonally, bite-size
 $\frac{1}{4}$ c. soy sauce
 $\frac{1}{4}$ c. sherry

2   tsp. corn starch
1   Tbs. Szechwan sauce
2   tsp. sesame oil
1   c. veg or chicken stock
    pinch red pepper flakes

Fry tofu in 2 Tbs. hot oil till brown, both sides. Remove; set aside. Add rest of oil to pan and heat. Stir in veggies, frying high heat, several minutes, stirring.

Mix together soy sauce, sherry, corn starch, sauce, sesame oil and stock together. Mix into veggies with noodles, mixing well. Stir in tofu, carefully. Heat till hot and serve with rice.

Tofu and Cashew Stir Fry
4-6 servings

2   Tbs. oil
3   Tbs. grated fresh ginger
1   lb. tofu, cut $\frac{1}{4}$"x $\frac{1}{2}$" x 2"
    strips
 $\frac{3}{4}$ lb. snow peas, ends trimmed
15   oz. can baby corn
1   c. unsalted, roasted cashews
    pieces or whole
1   c. stock
 $\frac{1}{4}$ c. soy sauce
 $\frac{1}{4}$ c. sherry
$1\frac{1}{2}$ tsp. cornstarch
1   tsp. sesame oil
    pepper to taste

Heat oil in heavy skillet. Fry half of tofu till golden brown, both sides. Stir in ginger, rest of tofu and pea pods. Fry high heat, several minutes, stirring.

Mix stock, soy sauce, cornstarch and sesame oil together. Add with cornstarch and cashews to tofu. Stir and cook till heated and thickened. Pea pods should be green and a little crisp.

Serve with rice.

Two-Bean Tofu Chile
6-8 servings

½ lb. pinto beans, soaked overnight and drained
2 lb. tofu, frozen overnight and thawed
6 Tbs. oil
1 lg. onion, chopped
½ c. quality chile powder
1 Tbs. oregano
2 tsp. cumin
1 tsp. marjoram
2 bay leaves
1 tsp. Tabasco
1 tsp. salt
1 16 oz. can tomatoes, with juice
1 6 oz. can tomato puree
3 c. vegetable bouillon
1 16 oz. garbanzos beans, drained

Cook soaked pintos in 4 c. water till just tender, 1½ hours, or so.

While beans are cooking, drain the frozen-defrosted tofu, which now looks like a sponge. Tear it in bite size pieces. (Now it doesn't look so bad) Pat dry.

Brown the onion first for 5 minutes, then add tofu, brown a few minutes and add seasonings and cook a few minutes more.

Add tomatoes, puree, bouillon and beans, including pintos. Cover and simmer an hour or more.

Vietnamese Lemon Grass Tofu
3-4 servings

1 lb. firm tofu, cut in bite-size cubes
2 stalks lemon grass
2 tsp. grated fresh ginger
2 cloves minced garlic
1 small fresh hot chile, seeded and minced, or ¼-½ tsp. hot pepper flakes
2 tsp. soy sauce
2 tsp. sugar
1 tsp. turmeric
1 tsp. curry powder
1 tsp. salt
2-3 Tbs. oil

Peel lemon grass to get to the tender inner parts. Mince tender inner stems. Mix lemon grass and rest of seasonings together. Add to tofu cubes in large bowl and gently mix well to coat tofu. Marinade ½ hour.

Heat oil in large skillet and carefully lay out tofu to cover bottom of skillet in one layer. Brown before turning and continue browning other sides.

Savory Tofu and Carrots
6-8 servings

4   medium-large carrots, grated
1   lb. tofu, crumbled
3   Tbs. butter
2   tsp. ground coriander
2   tsp. cumin
2   tsp. Spike seasoning salt
½   c. water
¼   c. soy sauce

Cook tofu in butter with spices for 5 minutes.

Add soy sauce, carrots and water. Mix well.

Cover and simmer till carrots are tender, 10-15 minutes.

Easy Millet Burgers
8-10 patties

Cook together, uncovered, for 25 minutes, until millet is cooked to a mush:

4   c. water
1   c. millet

Add and mix well while millet is still warm:

½   c. tahini or sesame butter
2   Tbs. soy sauce

2   tsp. Spike seasoning
♥   salt, pepper to taste

When cool, form into 8-10 patties. Fry in hot oil until browned both sides.

Serve on hamburger buns with "the works".

Tofu Sloppy Joes
4-6 buns worth

1   lb. tofu
2   Tbs. oil
1   Tbs. chili powder
2   Tbs. minced green pepper
2   Tbs. minced onion
2   Tbs. minced parsley
1   tsp. prepared mustard
1   c. water
¾   c. catsup

2   tsp. cider vinegar
2   tsp. brown sugar
♥   salt, pepper to taste

Heat oil and mash in tofu. Fry with chili powder and veggies, 5 minutes, on high.

Add rest and simmer 10 minutes. Serve over buns with fixin's.

Tofu Burgers
5-6 burgers

1   lb. tofu
1/3 c. quick cooking oats
1   Tbs. soy sauce
2   tsp. Worcestershire sauce
1   tsp. oregano
1   rubbed sage
½   tsp. thyme
½   tsp. paprika
     pinch rosemary
     salt, pepper to taste

Whip all ingredients together with electric mixer till it turns to a smooth paste. (It will!) Taste and adjust seasonings, as desired.

Form into patties and fry on a greased griddle. Or brush with oil and bake in oven at 375°, till crusty, 15-20 minutes.

Tofu "Meatballs"
16-20 meatballs

1   lb. tofu
2   slices bread, whole wheat
1   Tbs. Worcestershire sauce
1½   tsp. prepared brown
     mustard
1½   tsp. Spike seasoning salt
1   tsp. thyme
6   dashes Tabasco sauce

Put all in bowl and whip with electric mixer till it changes to a smooth paste, which it will.

Roll in walnut sized balls and fry in ½" hot oil. Or flatten slightly, brush with oil and bake at 375° for 15 minutes, till browned and firm.

Serve with different sauces and rice or pasta.

To serve as an appetizer, roll them smaller, fry and serve with a dipping sauce.

Scrambled Tofu
4-6 servings

3   Tbs. butter or oil
1   tsp. Spike seasoning salt
1½   c. small-chopped veggies,
     such as zucchini, green
     beans, sprouts, tomatoes
1   lb. tofu
¼   tsp. turmeric
1   tsp. cumin
2   Tbs. soy sauce

Heat butter and cook Spike in it a minute. Add veggies and simmer 8-10 minutes, till just tender. Squish and squeeze tofu out thru fingers into the pan. Increase heat, add turmeric, cumin and soy sauce and cook, mixing and stirring, 10 minutes, till bubbly.

Good for breakfast.

Flying Vegetables

Feathers

A big, busy mall is not the funnest place to work at any time, yet there I was, at the busiest season once again, selling gift items for Christmas, at a little concessions cart, in the middle of the holiday hubbub- but not necessarily the holiday cheer. (Something about Christmas shopping that brings out the "unresolved negative issues" in people.) It was night, after a long, intense day of frantic, needy people and no one showing up to take my shift. I was stuck, hungry, low on energy, and drained to the bottom of my soul, holding on for dear life until I could go home.

While helping customers I became aware of a young black girl standing near-by, holding a covered plate of food in her hand and patiently waiting for a space to open around me. She was beautiful in a tidy, quiet way, with dozens of small braids framing her face and wearing nice street clothing. And when she walked up to me it was like the rest of the mall just fell away and it was only her and me.

We said a few hello things to each other and then she handed me the plate, saying she wasn't hungry. I was amazed to be handed food and then to find it was my favorite repast from the food court (Way down at the other end of the mall): Cajun chicken with green beans and rice. I was thrilled, but that was just the start.

I put the plate by the cash register and happily turned to her once more (I remember customers standing by and watching.), and soon found myself holding her hands with our hands down at our sides, looking into her eyes, joyful and chirping like that open-hearted sweetness children have when they have found a loving friend. And as we stood there I remember feeling a huge surging of energy pouring into me from her hands, filling me like billowing clouds down to my feet and up, sustaining me, renewing my soul and my hope. She said her good-byes in a quiet way and I asked if I would see her again. She said, "yes," and I watched as she disappeared around a corner.

I never did see her again and even forgot her for awhile. But when I remembered, I marveled at what had been given me. Without fanfare my little mall angel had pulled me through a very hard time. Angels show up in the strangest places, even in malls. This chapter is dedicated to you, my mall angel. Your gifts live on.

Basic Roast Chicken

Whole, or pieces of chicken, washed, dried and oiled all over. Try mixing paprika with the oil before applying, for extra color and flavor.

I don't salt chicken until cooked as salt draws out the juices while cooking, but many cooks do salt. Your choice.

Place herbs, such as rosemary, sage, thyme, garlic inside the cavity, or stuff with a favorite stuffing or a peeled orange

Sprinkle pepper and favorite herbs such as oregano, marjoram, thyme, paprika, garlic, onion powder, liberally all over skin.

Place slivers of butter over top and even under the skin for moistness.

Bake at 300° for 1½ hours for a 3½ pound chicken, basting every 15-20 minutes. Let sit 15 minutes before cutting.

Chicken Fajitas
Serves 6

2	lbs. chicken breasts, boneless, skinless
1	c. Italian dressing (Good Seasons, from package)
½	c white wine, if desired
2-3	Tbs. Mexican Blend seasoning or other fajita seasoning
1	onion, halved, sliced thin
1	bell pepper, sliced thin
12	flour tortillas, warmed and set aside
1	recipe Fresh Mexican Salsa
1	recipe Guacamole
🌶	sour cream

Coat chicken well with Mexican seasoning. Marinate in dressing and wine overnight.

Grill over charcoal 5-8 minutes per side. Or broil in oven, or saute over low heat in pan. Baste well. Don't overcook. Slice into long strips and place on warmed platter.

Saute onion and pepper in a little oil, just till tender. Arrange over and/or around chicken strips.

To eat, fill each tortilla with chicken, veggies, salsa, sour cream and guacamole. Yum!

Almond Chicken
Serves 6-8

2½ to 3 lb. fryer, cut up and skinned

Spicy Almond Topping
- 1 c. blanched, chopped almonds
- 2" piece ginger, peeled and chopped
- 1 salt
- 1 tsp. paprika
- ½ tsp. ground coriander
- ½ tsp. cumin
- ½ tsp. pepper
- 1/3 c. oil or melted butter

Grind almonds and ginger in blender. Mix with all the spices. Brush chicken with oil or butter and roll in almond mixture.

Bake in ungreased pan at 325° about 50-60 minutes till thickest pieces just loose their pink when cut in middle.

Can use the almond mixture on casseroles and vegetables.

Tarragon Chicken
Serves 4

Tarragon is a powerful herb. Too much and it ruins the dish. Just enough and it supports and adds new dimension to an already existing divinity.

- 4 large chicken breasts, skinned and boned
- 4 green onions, chopped, or ½ c. chives, minced
- 4 tsp. butter
- ✐ pepper
- ☺ Parmesan cheese

Arrange chicken in small glass baking dish. Sprinkle onion and tarragon over tops. Dot each breast with 1 tsp. butter and sprinkle with pepper.

Pour around chicken:
- ½ c. dry white wine

Bake at 325° for 30-40 minutes, until it looses its pink in the thick part, when cut.

Cover each breast with following topping:

Whip until stiff:
- 1 egg white

Fold in:
- ½ c. mayonnaise

Sprinkle covered chicken generously with Parmesan. Return to oven and bake 10 minutes, until light brown.

Chicken Broiled with Pineapple Sauce
5-6 servings

1   lg. fryer chicken, cut up
¼   c. soy sauce

¾   c. pineapple juice
½   c. catsup
¼   c. lemon juice
2   Tbs. oil
1   Tbs. grated ginger, or
    1 tsp. powdered ginger
1   clove garlic, minced
🌶   pepper, to taste

Brush chicken all over with soy sauce, place in pan for broiling and let stand 30 minutes. Mix remaining ingredients in saucepan and bring to boil; then simmer for 30 minutes, to a thick sauce. Brush on chicken and broil 4" from flame at 350°. Baste frequently. Cook one side 20 minutes; turn and broil other side- more basting- 20 minutes.

Maui Chicken
Serves 6-8

This comes from Robin with the big family, among other gifts

3½ to 4 lbs. chicken pieces
4" ginger, peeled, sliced thin
½   c. soy sauce
½   c. sherry or white wine
1   medium onion, sliced thin
½   t. pepper

Mix all together in baking pan and marinate several hours or overnight. Bake at 325° for 45 minutes to 1 hour, turning and stirring several times.

Robin also has another version: Place the ginger and onion on bottom of pan with several cloves minced garlic. Arrange chicken in pan and sprinkle top of chicken with brown sugar and drizzle with soy sauce. Then bake. Gives it a bit of a glaze.

Easy, Spicy Baked Chicken
Serves 4

4   chicken breasts
2   Tbs. vinegar
1   Tbs. olive oil
1   Tbs. paprika
1   tsp. cumin seed, roasted
1   tsp. oregano
1   tsp. pepper
½   tsp. salt

Mix all together and spread over chicken in baking pan. Bake at 325° for 30-40 minutes, until it just looses it's pink when cut in the center.

Lemon Ginger Chicken
Serves 5-6

3½ to 4 lb. chicken pieces, skinned
¼ c. peeled ginger, cut up
1/3 c. soy sauce, or more
1 lemon, sliced thin (or try orange)
1 Tbs. sugar

Blend soy sauce and ginger together in blender. Mix in all the remaining ingredients. Marinate the chicken for several hours or overnight, covered, turning several times. Bake at 325° about 45 minutes, or broil, or barbecue!

Green Chile Chicken Enchilada
8-12 servings

Green chile is an important crop in New Mexico. At harvest time, big round metal roasting baskets can be found on many a street corner roasting chilies over an open flame. As the basket turns and chilies inside tumble while their skins char black, the rich smell fills the air and your car, as you whiz by and are lucky enough to have the windows rolled down. Green chile chicken enchilada casserole is a popular folk food- one of the many ways New Mexicans celebrate their green chilies. My dear friend, Rose, in Taos, gave me this recipe, which we had to decode (and make a few changes), as she was used to "just doing, not measuring ," and boiling a whole chicken for an hour or so and using the shredded meat.

3-4 chicken breasts
1 c. bouillon
 pinches rosemary, thyme
3 Tbs. butter
2 tsp. Spike seasoning salt
1 medium onion, chopped
4 cloves garlic, minced
2 c. sliced mushrooms (½lb.)
2 10 oz. cans cream of chicken soup concentrate
1 10 oz. can cream of mushroom soup concentrate
2 c. chopped green chile (frozen is good, drained)
16 corn tortillas
1 lb. jack cheese, grated

Simmer chicken breasts over low heat with herbs 15 minutes, until just done. Cool and cut into bite size pieces.

Saute Spike in butter and add veggies. Cook till just wilted.

Heat soups in ½ c. broth from chicken, smoothing out lumps. Add chicken, veggies, and chile.

Shred 8 tortillas onto bottom of deep 9"x12" pan. Pour ½ of chicken mix over all. Spread with half of cheese. Repeat with rest. Bake at 325° for 30-40 minutes, till bubbly and brown.

Mexican Bird
5-8 servings

3-4 lbs. chicken, cut and skinned
3 Tbs. oil
2 c. chicken stock
1 c. dry white wine
1 med. onion, cut in thin wedges
½ c. diced turkey ham
1/3 c. raisins
1 jalapeno, seeded, chopped
2 Tbs. minced parsley
2 Tbs. almonds, toasted, slivered
1 lg. clove garlic, minced
¼ tsp. cinnamon
½ tsp. ground coriander
½ tsp. cumin

handful green olives
pinch nutmeg

1 Tbs. corn starch, mixed with 1 Tbs. water

In large skillet, brown chicken in hot oil. Add stock and wine; bring to a boil. Mix all but cornstarch paste together and add to chicken. Reduce heat and simmer about 30 minutes, till juices are no longer pink.

Remove chicken from pan and stir cornstarch paste into stock and goodies. Stir till thickened. Serve over chicken on platter.

Chicken with Onions, Tomato, Olives and Wine
6 servings

4-6 chicken breasts, skinned
    juice of 1 lemon
2 tsp. thyme
½ tsp. pepper
6 Tbs. olive oil
3 onions, chopped fine
2 garlic cloves, minced
4-5 tomatoes, wedges
2 bay leaves
½ c. dry white wine
1 c. Kalamata olives
2 Tbs. minced fresh basil
☺ chopped parsley, garnish

Rub chicken with lemon, thyme and pepper. In heavy skillet, brown chicken in hot oil, about 5 minutes. Remove chicken; add onions. Brown 10 minutes. Add garlic, tomatoes, bay leaf, wine and cook 10 minutes.

Add chicken, olives and basil and cook slowly, uncovered, 25-30 minutes, basting and turning frequently. Salt to taste.

Serve sprinkled with parsley and perhaps some parmesan. Good with your favorite pasta.

Chicken and Vermicelli in Pepper Sauce
6 servings

3 lbs. chicken breasts, skinned, boned, cut in strips

16 oz. vermicelli twists, or egg noodles, cooked, hot

½ c. butter

2/3 c. Good Seasons Italian dressing, prepared from the package

3 Tbs. fresh lemon juice

1 Tbs. coarse or medium ground pepper (fine don't work so good)

¼ c. minced parsley

☺ Parmesan

Melt butter. Mix in salad dressing, lemon juice and pepper

Place chicken in a small glass baking dish and mix with sauce. Cover with tin foil, pierce in several places, and bake at 325° for about ½ hour, till just tender and no pink in middle. Mix with hot noodles in a pasta platter and sprinkle with parsley and Parmesan.

Try with jumbo shrimp and French bread rather then chicken and pasta.

Poached Chicken and Vegetables with Dumplings
6 servings

This bird has a quiet vegetable taste

1 whole chicken, 3½-4 lbs.

4 small leeks, chopped

2 large carrots, cut in 1" pieces on slant

½ lb. parsnip or celery root, 1" chunks

1 fennel bulb, cut 1" chunks

6 c. chicken stock or bouillon

2 dry white wine

4 bay leaves

1 tsp. thyme, or 2 big sprigs fresh

✎ salt, pepper, to taste

Stuff chicken with ½ the veggies and seal. Bring stock, wine and veggies to a boil. Add bird and simmer for 30 minutes, covered.

Add remaining veggies and simmer 30-45 minutes more, until all is tender. Remove all from broth and keep warm.

Mix together while chicken is cooking:

¼ c. flour

¾ c. matzo meal

2 tsp. baking powder

2 eggs

¼ c. milk

1 Tbs. oil

½ tsp. salt

¼ tsp. pepper

¼ c. minced parsley

Cover and refrigerate 30 minutes. Form into 1" balls and drop in simmering stock. Cover; simmer 15 minutes. Cut up chicken before serving.

Yogurt Chicken with Blackened Onions
Serves 4-6

Mix all together in non-metal bowl:

- 4 large chicken breast halves, skinned, bone in
- 1 c. plain, non-fat yogurt
- 1 onion, minced
- 2 tsp. whole cumin, dry roasted
- 1 tsp. rosemary leaves
- ½ tsp. turmeric
- ½ tsp. salt
- ¼ tsp. pepper
- ✍ pinch cayenne
- ✍ minced cilantro

Cover and refrigerate 3-4 hours. Place in non-metal baking dish and bake 20-25 minutes at 350°.

Drizzle:
- 1 tsp. olive oil over each piece

Place under broiler and cook 3-5 inches from flame for 5 minutes, or until onions begin to blacken and chicken is done. Garnish with fresh cilantro.

Chicken Breasts with Wine and Cream Sauce
4-6 servings

- ½ lb. broccoli or asparagus, bite-size pieces, steamed
- 4 chicken breasts, skinned and boned
- ♥ pepper
- 2 tsp. fresh lemon juice
- ♥ flour to dredge
- 2 Tbs. butter

Sauce:
- 2/3 c. chicken broth
- 2/3 c. Madeira or Sherry
- 2 c. whipping cream
- ½ tsp. salt
- ¼ tsp. pepper
- 1 tsp. lemon juice
- 2 Tbs. Parmesan cheese

Sprinkle each side of chicken with pepper and lemon juice and dredge in flour. Sauté chicken in butter 6-10 minutes on each side until chicken just looses it's pink. Set aside.

In pan used for chicken, add broth and wine and boil until reduced to 2/3 c., about 6-10 minutes. Add cream and reduce to 1¾ c., 12 minutes. Add lemon juice, salt, and pepper.

Place vegetables in bake ware with chicken on top. Pour sauce over chicken, sprinkle with Parmesan and broil at 375° for 4-5 minutes, till bubbly.

Chicken Paprika
6 servings

3 lbs. chicken, cut up, or 6 chicken breasts
4 Tbs. oil
1 onion, chopped fine
1 c. chopped parsley
1½ Tbs. paprika
   salt, pepper, to taste
1½ c. broth or bouillon
1 Tbs. flour
1 c. sour cream

Brown chicken and onions well in hot oil. Stir in parsley, seasonings and broth. Simmer, uncovered, till tender, about ½ hour, turning chicken a few times.

Remove chicken and keep hot on platter.

Make a paste with flour and a couple Tbs. water and stir into pan juices. Whisk over medium heat till thick and incorporated. Lower heat and stir in sour cream. Heat, but do not boil. Pour over chicken on serving platter and serve with thick noodles.

Can add ½ c. peas for color.

Make broth with chicken giblets, simmering in water for ½ hour, to use in the recipe.

Chicken in Brown Sauce
4-6 servings

3½ lbs. chicken, skinned and cut up
3 c. water or stock, bouillon
¼-½ tsp. hot red pepper flakes
¼ c. soy sauce
3 Tbs. flour
3 Tbs. toasted sesame seeds, ground, or 2 Tbs. tahini
1 tsp. sesame oil

Simmer chicken in stock and pepper flakes till tender, 30-40 minutes. Remove chicken from stock. Mix together soy sauce and flour and whisk into simmering stock with sesame seeds. Return chicken to pot, heat and simmer 10 minutes. Serve with rice.

Turkey Ham and Cheese Turnovers
6-8 large turnovers

To the Potato Cheese Turnover recipe add:
1-2 c. cubed turkey ham

Need I say more? The smoky ham flavor has a delicious influence.

Chicken in Plum Sauce
4 servings

2 chicken breasts, skinned boned, cut in 1" cubes
3 Tbs. dry white wine
2 Tbs. minced onion
2 Tbs. plum jam
1 Tbs. catsup
1 tsp. minced, fresh ginger
½ tsp. rice vinegar
½ tsp. salt
½ tsp. sugar

3 Tbs. oil
¼ c. chicken broth
1 Tbs. plum jam
1 tsp. cornstarch mixed with 1 Tbs. water

In a bowl, mix together white wine and rest down to sugar. Add chicken and marinade ½ hour to 8 hours, covered, in refrig.

Heat oil on high. Stir-fry chicken and marinade on high until chicken is almost cooked, about 2 minutes. Add chicken broth and 1 Tbs. plum jam and simmer 2-3 minutes.

Stir in cornstarch paste and stir till translucent and thickened.

Serve with rice and a green veg.

Walnut Chicken
4 servings

2 large chicken breasts, skinned, boned, cut in 1" cubes
1 tsp. cornstarch
1 tsp. water
1 egg white
¾ c. chopped walnuts
3 Tbs. soy sauce
2 Tbs. white wine
½ tsp. sugar
3 Tbs. oil
¼ c. small chopped celery
3 green onions, diagonal 2" slivers
2 tsp. fresh ginger, minced
1 garlic clove, minced

Whip together cornstarch, water and egg white. Add chicken and coat well. Combine soy sauce, wine and sugar and set aside.

Heat 2 Tbs. of oil in large skillet. Stir-fry chicken and walnuts 3-5 minutes until pink is gone from chicken and walnuts are toasted. Remove from pan.

Add rest of oil and celery, onions, ginger and garlic. Fry 1 minute. Add soy sauce mix and cook till thickened, a minute.

Try raw cashews instead of walnuts.

Curried Chicken with Coconut Milk
4-6 servings

4	chicken breasts, skinned and boned, cut in half
3	Tbs. butter
1	medium onion, chopped
½	lb. mushrooms, sliced
4	tsp. curry powder
2	tsp. grated or minced ginger
2	cloves garlic, minced
1½	Tbs. flour
1½	c. chicken stock
1	c. coconut milk (can find it in a can)
1	Tbs. red currant jelly
1	Tbs. orange juice concentrate
2	tsp. sugar
4	Tbs. cream

Melt butter in a large skillet. Add onions and mushrooms to skillet and saute till soft. Stir in curry, ginger and garlic and cook 3 minutes. Sprinkle on flour and cook a minute, stirring.

Whisk in stock, blending well. Add chicken and bring to boil. Turn down and then simmer 20 minutes, covered.

Blend in coconut milk, jelly, orange juice and sugar. Simmer 5 minutes. Stir in cream.

A delicate, rich subtle flavor.

Chipotle Roast Turkey Thighs
4-6 servings

These peppers are roasted jalapenos and they are fabulous. Makes your mouth water just smelling them. But you don't want to use too many as their fire power can put you in the next state. Blend the rest of the peppers in a blender and store in fridge and use to spice up other dishes. Makes an outstanding spread blended with mayo.

3-4	turkey thighs
3-5	chipotle peppers from a 7 oz. can Chipolte Peppers in Adobo Sauce
2	c. mango chunks (frozen is fine, but defrost a bit.)
1	Tbs. orange juice concentrate
1	tsp. balsamic vinegar
1	tsp. onion powder
½	tsp. garlic powder

Blend all but turkey together in blender to a smooth paste.

Wash, dry and oil turkey all over. Place in baking dish. Slather paste on non-skin side of turkey and place skin side up in pan. Slather more paste over skin side of turkey.

Bake in 325° oven for about 1 hour, or till juices run clear when thigh is cut.

Serve with rice. Sour cream will cut the heat, if too hot. Can use less chilies if you want it milder.

Roast Turkey with California Dressing
12-16 pound turkey

This is our favorite family turkey stuffer, which I've used ever since I discovered the recipe in a newspaper many long years ago when I was a teenager. Of course since then it's also become a nice vegetarian casserole dish – with or without cheese.

Prepare and set aside:
- 8 c. whole wheat bread, cut in 1" cubes

Saute together in large skillet:
- 4 Tbs. butter
- 2 stalks celery, chopped
- 1 large green pepper, diced
- 1 lg. onion, diced
- 1 bunch parsley, minced
- 2 tsp. whole sage
- 2 tsp. savory
- 1 tsp. oregano
- 1 tsp. thyme
- ½ tsp. rosemary
- 4 small bay leaves
- 1 tsp. salt
- ½ tsp. pepper

for 10-15 minutes. Scoop veggies into bowl, leaving juices in pan.

Add to skillet:
- ¼ c. butter
- 2 Tbs. olive oil

When hot, add bread cubes and quickly toss to coat bread evenly with melted butter-oil. Brown the bread in the skillet, turning to toast evenly

Add bread to vegetables, mixing well with:
- 1 c. chopped walnuts
- 1 6 oz. can black olives, crushed
- 1-2 chopped apples
- ¼ c. raisins

Stuff bird front and back. A crust of bread, stuffed in the cavity can seal the back. Butter the turkey all over with soft butter. Place in preheated oven at 500° for 20 minutes. Then lower heat to 325°. Follow baking time directions on wrapping of turkey. Baste every 20 minutes with pan drippings.

Try Currant Sauce brushed on the last 45 minutes as a glaze on turkey.

Any leftover stuffing that doesn't fit in bird can make a small casserole with added liquid and beans for protein, and cheese.

Turkey Moussaka (Baked Eggplant-Turkey Casserole)
9-12 servings

This is one of my favorites. In Albuquerque, the friendly neighborhood Greek restaurant serves this with a layer of sliced potato lining the bottom.

3   large eggplants, peeled and cut in ½" lengthwise slabs
½   c. olive oil
1   large onion, finely chopped
4   cloves garlic, minced
2   lbs. ground turkey
1½   c. tomato sauce
1   c. dry white wine
1   c. minced parsley
¼   tsp. nutmeg
½   tsp. cinnamon
☺   salt, pepper, to taste
1/3   c. bread crumbs
1½   c. Parmesan cheese
1   recipe Béchamel Sauce
♥   paprika

Brush each eggplant piece with oil, both sides. Arrange on cookie sheet and broil, turning, till fork tender.

Heat rest of oil, about ¼ c., in skillet and saute onions and garlic at low heat 5-8 minutes. Add turkey and brown, breaking it up with a fork.

Stir in tomato sauce, wine, parsley and seasonings. Simmer 15-20 minutes more. Adjust salt and pepper.

To assemble:

Sprinkle greased 10"x14" glass or enamel baking pan with bread crumbs. Arrange half the eggplant in the bottom of pan. Sprinkle with ½ c. Parmesan. Spread turkey evenly over eggplant and top with remaining eggplant. Sprinkle with ½ c. Parmesan. Spread Béchamel Sauce evenly over top; sprinkle with remaining cheese and dust with parmesan and paprika.

Bake at 350° for 1 hour or till golden brown and puffed. Cool 20 minutes before cutting.

Try a layer of boiled, sliced potato, sprinkled with paprika, as the bottom layer of the casserole. An awesome dish, either way.

Rio Grande Chili
6-8 servings

6 Tbs. oil
1 large onion, chopped
3 garlic cloves, minced
2 lb. ground turkey
½ c. chili powder
1 Tbs. oregano leaf
2 tsp. cumin seed, roasted
1 tsp. marjoram
2 bay leaves
1 tsp. Tabasco sauce
1 tsp. salt
¼ tsp. red pepper flakes
1 16 oz. can whole tomatoes, with juice, crushed
½ c. tomato puree
3 c. bouillon, or stock
½ lb. dry pinto beans, soaked overnight in water to cover
4 c. water

Brown onions and garlic in hot oil, covered, at low heat, 10 minutes. Add turkey and seasonings and brown, breaking up the turkey with fork. Add tomatoes, puree, and stock. Cover and simmer very slowly an hour.

While chili is cooking, drain beans, add water, bring to a boil, turn down and simmer till beans are tender, about 1-1½- hours.

Add beans to chili and simmer another hour.

Turkey Curry
Serves 6-8

3 Tbs. oil
1 lb. ground turkey
1 medium onion, chopped
2 medium potatoes, diced
1 green pepper, diced
2 Tbs. grated fresh ginger
1 tsp. curry powder
1 tsp. chili powder
1 tsp. cumin, ground
¼ tsp. turmeric
¼ tsp. cardamom, ground
¼ tsp. cinnamon
☺ salt, pepper, to taste

2 Tbs. tomato paste
2½ c. water or stock

In a large skillet over medium heat, brown the turkey and vegetables. Stir in seasonings and cook a few minutes. Mix in tomato paste and water. Heat to boiling, reduce heat, and simmer, uncovered, until vegetables are tender and sauce is thickened, 20-30 minutes.
Serve with rice and chutney.

Spicy Turkey Sausage with Gravy
5 patties

Gravy
2	c.	water or stock
3	Tbs.	soy sauce
5	Tbs.	flour
1	tsp.	onion salt
1	tsp.	paprika
✐		pinch allspice
✐		pepper, to taste

Whisk all together in saucepan
over medium heat till thickened

Sausage
1	lb.	ground turkey
2	tsp.	onion powder
1½	tsp.	cumin powder
1	tsp.	ground coriander
1	tsp.	sage leaf, crumbled

½	tsp.	Oregano
½	tsp.	Paprika
½	tsp.	Marjoram
¼	tsp.	Thyme
¼	tsp.	Fennel
½	tsp.	Salt
¼	tsp.	Pepper
☺		pinch rosemary
☺		pinch mace

Mix all together well (I squish
between my fingers). Form into
patties and fry, low heat, till firm
and done in middle.

Turkey shrinks a lot as it cooks so
make patties oversized and thin.
Serve with gravy.

Turkey Sloppy Joes
4-6 buns worth
Flavorful and easy. Kids go for it.

1	lb.	ground turkey
1	Tbs.	oil
¾	c.	catsup
2	Tbs.	minced green pepper
2	Tbs.	minced parsley
2	Tbs.	minced green onion, if desired
1	Tbs.	chili powder
½	Tbs.	prepared mustard
1	c.	water or stock
1	Tbs.	brown sugar
2	tsp.	vinegar
½	tsp.	salt
☺		pepper, to taste

Heat skillet with oil and fry turkey
on medium heat until brown,
breaking up the pieces with a fork,
while cooking.

Add vegetables towards end of
frying and cook 5 minutes. Add
rest of ingredients and simmer till
well blended and hot.

Serve in hamburger buns with a
sprinkling of cheese and whatever
else you desire.

Succulent Sides

If the Shoe Fits

As the story goes from my Aunt Charlotte, my Grandma Mimi was also a busy cook. Raised in Regensburg, Germany, she came from a family known to be the shoe-makers to some Royal Family. As my Aunt says, my Grandma was being groomed to be the bride of the mayor of the town, which meant learning to handle a large estate in all its aspects.

Thus, she spent several years at various island resorts getting trained in deportment, and was on her way to a culinary school in South Dakota (of all places!) when her heart was waylaid by an itinerant artist (my grandfather!), also from Germany. They were married, and that was the end of her dreams of career, if ever they were her dreams.

She was a splendid cook, and took care of her family of six with warmth and graciousness. My uncle says I remind him of her, and that suits me fine. She was an earthy lady, too, and would blame the dog for various indiscretions. She did not hoist fine manners on me, but rather gave me personal examples of patience and generous forgiveness, which I took to heart as soon as they were given.

My Russian grandma was also Jewish and Austrian, which takes away some of the Russian, I suppose. But I relate well to the heroic and poignant quality of that flavor of mankind, and thus hold cabbage and beets in due honor and respect.

I have made both borscht and cabbage snails and tofu-mushroom pirogues for Russian visitors here. Reports coming back say all was much appreciated, and tribute was given, of which you will have to guess!

Golden Rice
4-6 servings

Saute:
2   Tbs. butter
½   c. cashews
½   c. shredded carrot

Add:
1   c. rice, long grain
1   c. apple juice
1   c. water
½   c. golden raisins

1   Tbs. brown sugar
½   tsp. salt
½   tsp. curry powder
¼   tsp. cinnamon
¼   tsp. ginger

Bring to a boil, reduce heat to lowest setting. Cover and cook for 20 minutes. (Don't lift the lid!)

Sweet and tasty!

Lemon Rice
4-6 servings

1   c. rice, long grain
2   Tbs. butter
1   tsp. black mustard seed
½   tsp. turmeric
½   tsp. salt
2   c. water
2   Tbs. fresh lemon juice

Heat butter and stir in mustard seed till it starts popping. Add rice and remaining seasonings, stirring a few moments. Add water. Bring to a boil, cover and turn heat to lowest setting. Cook 20 minutes. Toss with lemon juice.

Succulent Rice
4-6 servings

1   c. rice, long grain
2   c. chicken broth or
    vegetable substitute

Add your choice of:
♥   minced parsley
♥   chopped green olives
♥   chives
♥   green pepper
♥   ample black pepper
♥   salt

Add what ingredients you want with rice and broth. Bring to a boil, cover tightly, and turn to lowest heat. Cook 20 minutes.

Don't lift the lid during the steaming process or the rice will sog.

Greek Rice Pilaf
5-6 servings

Unusual smoky, good flavor, created by my friend Carol, who made beautiful party settings

1	c. rice
2	Tbs. butter
1	Tbs. olive oil
1	tsp. marjoram
¼	c. pine nuts
1/3	c. currants
1/3	c. minced grape leaves
¼	c. sliced stuffed green olives
♥	pepper
2	c. water

Saute rice and pine nuts in butter and oil till lightly browned. Add rest of ingredients, bring to a boil, cover, turn to lowest heat, and steam till tender, 20 minutes.

Grape leaves and olives might be enough salt, but check.

(Grape leaves can be found bottled in brine. Unroll and rinse 2-4 leaves, stack and mince.)

Wild Rice Stuffing
Stuff a 12 lb. turkey or make a side for 6

Tastes nourishing and uniquely flavorful.

If preparing for a turkey:
Prepare giblets by washing and cutting; simmer, covered, for ½ hour with:
4½ c. water
1 tsp. salt
Add:
1½ c. wild rice

Cover and simmer until tender, for 30-40 minutes. Remove giblets.

If going vegetarian, substitute vegetable bouillon for the giblets, and start with the rice.

Saute in skillet 5 minutes:
3 green onions, chopped
1 small tart apple, chopped
½ c. chopped celery
½ c. chopped, sliced water chestnuts
2 Tbs. minced parsley
2 tsp. minced green pepper
1 bay leaf
♥ pepper
♥ garlic powder, if desired
♥ onion powder, if desired

Add rice and chopped liver from giblets. Add rest of seasonings. Either stuff a turkey, or heat and serve. Try adding pine nuts.

Spanish Rice with a Kick
6-8 servings

2	Tbs. vegetable oil
2	Tbs. butter
½	c. minced onion
¼	c. minced green pepper
2	c. long grain rice
4	c. water
¼	c. medium-hot chili powder
1	tsp. oregano
1	tsp. marjoram
1	tsp. salt
1	large tomato, chopped fine

In saucepan, heat oil and butter and saute onion and green pepper over medium heat till soft, 5-6 minutes. Add remaining ingredients and bring to a boil. Cover; reduce heat to lowest point and steam 20 minutes. Stir in tomato the last 10 minutes.

Fluff up before serving. Garnish with cilantro.

Pulao- East Indian Pilaf
4-6 servings
A delicate, savory rice

4	Tbs. ghee or butter
1	c. basmati rice
2¼	c. water
¾	c. cubed eggplant
½	c. peas
¼	c. chopped sweet pepper
¼	c. pistachios or chopped almonds
¼	c. cashews
2	Tbs. raisins
1	tsp. turmeric

2	cinnamon sticks or
	½ tsp. cinnamon
1	tsp. salt
¼	tsp. ground cardamom

Heat ghee and add rice. Stir frequently until lightly browned. Add water; bring to a boil. Add spices and all the goodies. Bring back to a boil, cover, and cook at lowest heat, 20 minutes.

Roasted Potato Wedges

Using 1 medium baking potato per person, cut each potato into 8 wedges. Brush each wedge with olive oil and roll in a mix of minced garlic or garlic powder and your favorite seasoning salt and pepper. Place in a glass baking dish in a single, separated layer and bake at 400° for 25-30 minutes, until lightly browned and tender.

Try sprinkling and tossing with parmesan cheese and baking a few more minutes.

Potato Cheese Puffs
8 servings

Good "meat and potato" type dish

4	medium to large potatoes, 2 lbs., freshly boiled
¼	c. cream
2	eggs, separated
1	c. grated onion
1	tsp. salt
1	tsp. onion powder
2	Tbs. minced parsley

Whip egg whites stiff. Whisk milk, egg yolks, cheese, parsley and seasonings in a bowl. Drain hot potatoes and add to milk. Whip till creamy and fluffy with mixer. Fold in egg whites.

On greased cookie sheet form 8 round mounds. Bake at 425°, 15-20 minutes. Serve pronto.

New Potatoes with Herbs and Parsley
4-5 servings

1½	lbs. new potatoes, steamed tender, cut in chunks
¼	c. butter, or 2 Tbs. olive oil and 2 Tbs. butter
½	c. minced parsley
½	c. minced fresh herbs, such as: thyme, oregano, savory
	salt, pepper, to taste

Saute potatoes in butter at medium-high heat, browning and turning. Add parsley and herbs. Brown 5 or so minutes more. Add salt and pepper.

Also good sautéed with Spike and fresh mushrooms.

Creamy Potatoes and Peas
6-8 servings

6	c. diced potatoes, steamed tender
2	c. frozen peas
¼	c. butter
2	Tbs. grated onion
2	tsp. Spike, seasoning salt
¼	tsp. pepper
1	c. grated cheese of your choice
1	c. sour cream

Melt butter; stir in seasonings. Cook a minute or so. Blend in cheese and sour cream. Add potatoes and peas and mix well.

Pour into a buttered casserole dish and bake at 350° for 20-25 minutes, till hot.

This is something I made up when I was a teenager.

Potato Latkes
24 pancakes

6 potatoes, peeled and grated
1 small onion, grated
3 eggs
¼ c. flour or matzo meal
1 tsp. salt
½ tsp. pepper
½ c. oil or butter

Grate potatoes and onions. Place in large wire colander and squeeze well to drain. Beat eggs and add to potatoes with flour and seasonings. Drop from spoon into hot oil in large skillet. Brown one side before turning to brown other.

Yeast Potato Pancakes
8 pancakes

1 Tbs. grated onion
1 Tbs. oil
2 pkg. active dry yeast
1 c. warm milk or bouillon
1 large, raw potato, grated
1 egg, beaten
2/3 c. flour
1 tsp. Spike seasoning salt
1 tsp. salt
 pepper

Saute onion in oil a few minutes. Soften yeast in liquid, 5 minutes. Stir in grated potato, seasoning, egg, flour and onion with oil.

Let rise ½ hour. Stir down. Drop on lightly greased griddle and brown on each side over medium heat, about 6-7 minutes. Serve with applesauce and yogurt or sour cream.

Curried Potatoes
4-6 servings

3 large potatoes
1 large onion, ¼" cubes
1 Tbs. grated ginger
½ fresh green chile, minced, or ¼-½ hot pepper flakes
3 Tbs. oil
1 tsp. black mustard seeds
1 tsp. turmeric
½ tsp. salt
½ lemon, juice of
 chopped cilantro

Steam potatoes tender. Cut in small cubes. Heat oil and add mustard seeds. When finished popping, add onions and ginger. Saute until soft. Add chile, turmeric and potatoes with about ½ cup water. Cook and stir until mixture cooks dry, seasoning with salt. Blend in cilantro and lemon juice and serve.

Curried Potato Turnovers
6-8 turnovers

2	lbs. potatoes, cooked and cubed
¼	c. butter or ghee
2	tsp. black mustard seed
2	Tbs. grated fresh ginger
1	Tbs. ground cumin
2	tsp. marjoram
2	tsp. turmeric
1	tsp. onion powder
1	tsp. salt, or to taste
¼	tsp. pepper, or to taste
½	c. water, or stock
1½	c. peas

Add mustard seed to hot butter and when they start to pop, stir in rest of spices. Stir and cook 1 minute. Add potatoes and peas, mixing well. Cool completely.

Follow directions for making turnovers in Spinach Turnovers recipe.

To serve as a vegetable without the turnover part, continue cooking 10-15 minutes.

Banana Curry
4-5 servings

Unique and very flavorful

3	Tbs. butter
1	tsp. black mustard seed
1	Tbs. grated fresh ginger
1	tsp. ground cumin
1	tsp. ground coriander seed
1	tsp. turmeric
½	tsp. ground cardamom
1/3	tsp. cinnamon
1/3	tsp. nutmeg
4	whole cloves
☺	pinch cayenne
1	tsp. salt
1	c. plain yogurt
2	c. water
3	Tbs. garbanzo (besan) flour
5	bananas, sliced diagonally

Cook mustard seed and ginger in hot butter in skillet till mustard seed begins to pop. Add rest of spices and cook a few minutes, stirring.

Make a paste with besan flour and a little of the water. Add to spices in pan with yogurt and rest of water. Whisk smooth. Cook over medium heat, stirring, until thick and bubbly.

Add bananas and heat just until hot, 5-8 minutes. If cooked too long they loose their plumpness and savor.

Makes a delicious sauce over rice.

Banana Sweet Potato Casserole
6 servings

Different and delicious!

3 medium 6"sweet potatoes or yams, baked or steamed tender, not mushy
3 large bananas
3-4 Tbs. butter
½ c. maple syrup, brown sugar or honey
½ c. fresh (if possible) orange juice

Cool, peel and slice sweet potatoes, ½". In buttered baking dish, alternate a layer of sweet potato- sprinkled with salt and dotted with butter- with a layer of sliced banana- drizzled with sweetener- twice, 4 layers total.

Pour orange juice over all. Bake at 350° for 30 minutes.

Sweet Potato Pie
One 9" pie

½ recipe Pie Crust
2 lbs. sweet potatoes or yams steamed or baked tender
1/3 c. sugar or other sweetener
3 Tbs. butter
1 c. whipping cream or half & half
2 eggs
☺ large pinch each of nutmeg, cardamom, salt and pepper

Peel sweet potatoes and mash potatoes by hand or electric mixer. Add sugar, butter, cream, eggs and seasonings.

Pour into unbaked pie shell. Sprinkle more nutmeg on top and bake at 375° about 35-40 minutes, until knife inserted in center comes out clean.

Candied Sweet Potato or Yams
6-8 servings

3 lbs. baked sweet potatoes, peeled and cut in big chunks
½ c. butter
1 c. brown sugar
¼ c. orange juice concentrate
☺ salt

Melt butter in a large, heavy skillet. Add sugar and orange juice and cook, stirring, a few minutes. Add potatoes, spreading them out among the sweet stuff, and let cook on one side about 5-8 minutes before turning to cook others sides.

Salt and serve with all the sweet goo. Good without orange juice, also.

Fancied Sweet Potato or Winter Squash

Take steamed or baked sweet potatoes, yams or winter squash, peel and mash with butter, maple syrup/brown sugar and cardamom and a little cream to create a quick and easy special touch. Serve hot!

Winter Squash with Apple
6-8 servings

1   medium butternut squash,
    2 lbs., halved, seeded,
    peeled, cut in ½" cubes
1   large, glistening apple,
    like gala or gold Delicious,
    peeled, cored, cubed same
4   Tbs. butter
1   tsp. Spike, seasoning salt
1   tsp. cinnamon
♥   a few cloves
1   c. water
4   Tbs. maple syrup, or brown
    sugar, packed
2   tsp. fresh lemon juice
🖊   salt, pepper

Melt butter in large skillet and add Spike, cooking a minute. Add squash, cloves, cinnamon and cook 5 minutes. Add water, cover tightly, and simmer 10 minutes. Add apple and simmer 5-10 minutes more, until all is tender and water is cooked down.

Stir in maple syrup, lemon juice, salt and pepper, to taste. Heat well and serve sprinkled with nutmeg.

Glazed Carrots
4-5 servings

6   c. carrot fingers, or use
baby carrots (about 1 lb.)

To cut carrots into fingers, cut them in half, lengthwise. Turn the cut side down on board and slice at a sharp angle, making long fingers.)

3   Tbs. butter or ghee
3   Tbs. brown sugar
4   Tbs. apple juice concentrate
¾   c. water
½   tsp. turmeric
½   tsp. ground cardamom
1   tsp. coriander
½   tsp. salt

Mix all ingredients with carrots in large, heavy skillet. Bring to a boil, cover, and simmer at low heat until tender. When only a little water is left, uncover and at medium heat boil away the rest, stirring to keep all from sticking, until only a shiny glaze on carrots remains.

Mix into glazed carrots and serve:
♥   pepper, to taste
2   Tbs. chopped cilantro
1   tsp. fresh lime or lemon
    juice

Cabbage Snails
4-6 servings

Delightful, flavorful little critters that bake up well for company. My daughter asks for these.

8 c. fine chopped cabbage (½ of medium)
3 Tbs. butter
1 tsp. black mustard seed
1 tsp. cumin seed
2 tsp. Spike, seasoning salt
½ tsp. paprika
½ tsp. dill
¼ tsp. dry mustard
¼ tsp. pepper
¼ c. water

1 tsp. red wine vinegar
8 sheets fillo dough, thawed according to package directions, kept covered
½ c. butter, melted and hot

Melt the 3 Tbs. butter in a large skillet. Add mustard seed and cook till they start popping. Stir in rest of spices and cook a minute. Mix in cabbage; cover and cook a few minutes. Add water and vinegar and mix all well. Simmer till crunchy tender, 10-12 minutes.

Cool completely. Divide the cooled cabbage into 8 equal portions right in skillet.

Unroll thawed fillo. Loosen top sheet, without removing it from pile. Brush well with melted butter. At the bottom edge, lengthwise, arrange one portion of cabbage along the edge, making the row 1" wide. Roll cabbage up in a tight roll, making 1 long tube. Transfer to cookie sheet and roll into a tightish spiral. Don't mind if the fillo breaks a bit as you bend it. Just push it together and push tight against edge of cookie sheet. Butter all around. Make rest of snails, buttering outside and move them close together to hold contents in.

Bake at 425° for 20-30 minutes, until golden brown. Last 10 minutes of baking, separate them so they can brown all around.

Colcannon
4-6 servings

Traditional Irish folk food, only I don't peel them- what a waste!

1½ lbs. potatoes, 4 medium, cut up and cooked tender
1¼ c. milk
3 c. shredded cabbage
1 c. bouillon
2-3 Tbs. grated onion, or ¾ c. minced leeks
1 Tbs. minced parsley
4 Tbs. butter
☺ salt, pepper, to taste

Simmer cabbage in the bouillon, covered, till tender (water will be cooked away). Drain. In separate pan, melt 2 Tbs. butter and cook onions or leeks till wilted. Add milk and parsley and heat. While potatoes are still hot, whip them with the milk till fluffy. Mix in cabbage and seasonings. Mound potatoes on platter, indent top to cradle rest of butter, and serve.

Mex Mix
4-6 servings

1 lb. green beans, cut in half
1 large potato, cut in chunks
¼ c. olive oil
1 large tomato, cut in thin wedges and those halved
1 small red pepper, roasted, cut in thin strips
1 small green pepper, cut in thin strips
½ c. corn
1-2 pickled jalapenos, chopped

1 tsp. Spike seasoning salt
2 tsp. marjoram leaf
½ c. water or stock
☺ salt, pepper, to taste

Steam green beans and potatoes till almost tender. Heat oil in skillet; add vegetables and seasoning with stock. Simmer, uncovered, 10 minutes, till blended and tender.

Corn Fritters with Mexican Fixin's
12 large cakes

Plain fritters:
- 2½ c. fresh or frozen corn kernels
- 3 eggs, separated
- 3 Tbs. flour
- ¼ c. milk
- ☺ salt, pepper, to taste

Fixin's- pick any or all:
- 1-2 Tbs. chopped pickled jalapenos
- 2 Tbs. minced green or red bell pepper
- 3-4 Tbs. chopped green chilies
- 2 green onions, fine chopped, or 2 Tbs. minced onion

Whip egg whites stiff. Set aside. Beat all else together. Fold in egg whites. Drop by spoonfuls on hot, oiled griddle and brown on both sides.

Serve with butter or sour cream. Good with hot syrup. Try them with a chutney, salsa, or good just plain.

Braised Eggplant in Brown Sauce
4-5 servings

- 1 medium eggplant, peeled and cut in planks
- 3 Tbs. oil
- 2 cloves garlic, minced
- ¾ c. stock or bouillon
- ¼ c. sherry
- 3 Tbs. soy sauce
- 1 Tbs. corn starch
- 1 tsp. Hoisin sauce (Chinese section of grocery store)
- ¼ tsp. pepper

Heat oil hot. Stir in eggplant and garlic and cook at high heat, stirring, several minutes. Add stock and sherry; stir and cook until eggplant is tender, 5-10 minutes.

Mix cornstarch with soy sauce and add to eggplant with Hoisin and pepper. Stir till thickened. Adjust seasonings.

Tangy Beets
4-6 servings

3   large beets, cooked,(see Borscht recipe) diced, hot
1-2   Tbs. butter
2   Tbs. vinegar
1   Tbs. brown sugar
2   Tbs. orange juice concentrate
1   tsp. Worcestershire sauce
½   paprika
½   tsp. salt
¼   tsp. dry mustard
¼   tsp. cloves

In saucepan, mix all ingredients together except beets, melting butter and blending all. Add beets and coat well. Serve hot.

To serve cold, substitute oil for butter and cool before serving.

Baby Peas and Almonds
Serves 6-8

4   Tbs. butter
1   tsp. Spike seasoning salt
1/3   c. almonds, chopped
1   lb. frozen petit peas
  pepper, to taste

Saute almonds with Spike in butter till brown. Stir in peas. Cover and simmer 5-7 minutes, till hot. Season and serve.

Puree of Pea
2-4 servings

3   c. fresh or frozen green peas
½   c. cream
2-3   Tbs. butter
  salt, pepper, to taste

Simmer peas in a little water till tender, 8-10 minutes. Drain.

Blend with cream to a smooth paste in blender. Return to pan and reheat with butter, salt and pepper. Should be thick enough to blop from a spoon. Add more cream to thin or cook longer to thicken.

Green Bean Vinaigrette

Serve beans steamed, or simmered in bouillon, and then tossed with your favorite Italian or vinaigrette dressing. Serve at room temperature.

Green Beans and Almonds
Serves 5-6

2 Tbs. butter
1/3 c. almonds, whole, blanched
1 lb. trimmed green beans
1 tsp. Spike seasoning salt
1 c. water
1 cube bouillon

Heat butter in skillet. Add almonds and brown over low heat, stirring. Remove almonds from pan, leaving butter. Add green beans and Spike and brown a few minutes. Add water and bouillon, cover and simmer till tender. Remove beans to a serving platter and keep hot. Boil juices down to half their volume. Pour over beans and sprinkle with almonds.

Green Beans and Kalamatas
Serves 6

1 pound green beans, cut in half or thirds
10 Kalamata olives, sliced off pits, lengthwise
½ red pepper, roasted, strips
1/3 c. minced red onion
2 Tbs. vinegar of choice
3 Tbs. olive oil
☺ salt and pepper to taste

Steam green beans just until tender, 7-8 minutes. Turn out hot into bowl and add rest of ingredients. Mix well. Serve.

Green Beans, Artichoke Hearts and Feta Saute
4-6 servings

1 lb. green beans, trimmed into 1" pieces
2 Tbs. olive oil
1 small onion, minced
1 15 oz. can artichoke hearts, drained and chopped
½ c. vegetable or chicken bouillon or broth
2 Tbs. fresh lemon juice
½ c. or more, feta cheese
✒ salt, pepper, to taste

Heat olive oil in a saute pan. Add green beans and onion and saute 3 minutes. Stir in artichoke hearts and saute a little more.

Add broth; cover and simmer till beans are tender and broth is cooked down to half the volume. Stir in lemon juice, feta and salt and pepper. Serve warm.

Family Style Green Beans

Green beans are great just steamed until barely tender-not mushy- and tossed with butter, salt, pepper. It brings out the best in them.

Zucchini with Artichoke Hearts and Feta

Substitute zucchini for green beans in the recipe Green Beans, Artichoke Hearts and Feta Saute. Use a little less water.

Fried Zucchini Cakes
17-20 cakes

Mix all together:
- 4 c. grated zucchini
- 2 Tbs. grated fresh ginger
- 2 Tbs. grated green pepper
- 2 Tbs. grated onion, if desired
- 4 Tbs. chopped fresh cilantro
- 1 tsp. salt
- ½ tsp. baking powder
- ẽ pinch cayenne
- 1½ c. garbanzo flour (also called besan, the finest kind of garbanzo flour)

Fry by the spoonful in ½" hot oil in a heavy fry pan, at medium-high heat, turning to brown both sides well.

Serve with Mustard Lemon Sauce
Mix all together:
- ½ c. mayonnaise or yogurt
- 2 tsp. Dijon mustard
- 1 Tbs. fresh lemon juice

Zucchini with Tomato
4-5 servings

- 2 lbs. zucchini (5-6 medium), cut in ½" slices
- 1 medium tomato, cubed
- 4 Tbs. olive oil
- 1 tsp. Spike seasoning salt
- 1 tsp. oregano leaf
- ẽ minced fresh basil
- ẽ pepper, to taste

Heat oil. Add Spike and oregano; stir a minute. Add veggies; mix well. Cover and cook till tender, stir a few times, 10-15 minutes.

Creamed Spicy Spinach
6 servings
A heavily spiced spinach that bursts into flavor in your mouth. This dish is what my son wants every holiday

3   10 oz. pkg. frozen chopped spinach, defrosted, not drained, or 2 lbs. fresh spinach, trimmed, washed and chopped
4-5   Tbs. butter

Combine in small bowl:
1½   tsp. ground ginger or 2 Tbs. fresh grated
2   tsp. ground cumin
2   tsp. ground coriander
1½   tsp. sweet garam masala, or pumpkin pie spice with added pepper
1   tsp. onion powder
½   tsp. salt
½   tsp. garlic
½   tsp. turmeric
1/3   tsp. mace or allspice

½   c. sour cream, yogurt, cream cheese, or cream

Melt butter in large skillet. Add spices and cook, stirring, a minute or two.

Add spinach. If fresh, cover and cook over low heat a few minutes until melted down a bit. Turn and mix. Cook a few minutes more until well heated. Stir in cream of your choice and reheat. Don't simmer. Adjust salt. Serve hot.

Cauliflower and Mustard Seed
5-6 servings

1   cauliflower, trimmed and chopped fine, size of peas
2-3   Tbs. oil
2   tsp. black mustard seed
🥄   salt, pepper, cayenne, to taste

Heat oil, add mustard seed, and when they start popping add cauliflower. Cook over medium-low heat, stirring now and then. When it starts to get too dry but brown, 10 minutes, add ½ c. water and cook some more. One more time add water and cook- should be tender and seasoned with pan juices. Salt and pepper, to taste.

Broccoli with Lemon
6-8 servings

1   large bunch broccoli
2   Tbs. olive oil
2   Tbs. butter
☺   juice of 1 lemon, freshly squeezed
☺   salt, pepper

Wash and peel the woody outsides of stems of broccoli. The insides are tender and tasty. Cut in half, lengthwise, and then cut $\frac{1}{2}$" pieces crosswise at a slant till you reach the bud portions. Separate the buds into smaller pieces by cutting them in half lengthwise.

Steam broccoli till crisp-tender. Immediately remove lid to preserve fresh green color.

Melt butter and oil together and add lemon juice. Pour over broccoli in serving bowl and toss to mix with salt and pepper.

Nutty Baked Tomatoes
8 servings

4   tomatoes, cut in half and arranged in baking dish cut side up

Nut-Crumb Topping:
Brown all together in skillet:
2   Tbs. butter
2   Tbs. olive oil
2   tsp. Spike seasoning salt
1   Tbs. basil leaves
1   tsp. oregano
$\frac{1}{2}$ c. walnuts, chopped fine

Add:
$\frac{1}{4}$ c. cracker or bread crumbs
$\frac{1}{2}$ c. Parmesan cheese

Mound nut mixture over tomato halves. Bake at 350° for 30 minutes, or until tender when pierced with a fork.

If using less tomatoes, store leftover topping in fridge and use for other dishes. Tasty.

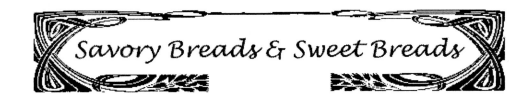

Savory Breads & Sweet Breads

Staff of Life

Mother Earth gives us our home and everything that's in it, including "the amber waves of grain." My son, David, age 14 at the time, is the poet. –
I'll let him say it:

"Mother"
Open our eyes to our graceful, beautiful Mother, more beautiful if we realize
And see Her pleading gaze.– Not from Her eyes
From the eyes of the people, who care, and love Her.
Here, we will not rest upon the earth, until we open our eyes.

"Life"
Dancing with life of the world, our Mother; sheltering them with hope;
Guarding them with fury,
So not a one predator would harm them.
Believe them, not kill them, love them, not hate them,
Worship their life as you worship yours. You are no different than they are.
Living upon the waves of life, dolphins, born of spirit and grace.
Guard them; love them, not harm them

"Goddess"
Rain clouds drifting across the sky, laying to sleep a golden sphere-
Only to our eyes.
Alive with belief in their Goddess: A Goddess that not only dances in their eyes,
But in their lives.
They are the graceful messengers of the gods, brought to this earth to keep the balance of Life and Death.
Howl with might upon night.
Rain clouds drifting across the sky
Alive with life.

"Sourdough" Bread
2 loaves
You don't need a starter for this, to get a taste similar to the "real thing"

2   pkg. active dry yeast
1½ c. warm water (105°-115°)
1   Tbs, sugar
1   c. plain yogurt
3   tsp. salt
5½-6 c. flour

Dissolve yeast and sugar in water in large bowl. Add yogurt, salt, and 3 c. flour. Blend 3 minutes with beater, medium speed. Stir in 2 c. flour by hand to make a stiff dough. Knead bread using rest of flour up to 1 c., until dough is smooth and elastic, about 5-8 minutes. When you poke it, it springs back at you.

Place in oiled bowl, turn so all surfaces are oiled. Cover and let rise in a warm place, till doubled, about 1 hour.

Cut dough in half and shape into rounds- (pressing and pulling under to make a smooth roundness on top). Let rise on greased cookie sheet, till doubled- warm place, no drafts - about 30 minutes.

Cut 3 slashes across top. Brush or spray with water. Bake at 375° for 35-45 minutes, spraying with water every 10-15 minutes, until loaves sound hollow when tapped.

Multi-grain Molasses Whole Wheat Country Bread
2 round loaves

2   c. warm water
2   pkg. active dry yeast
1   Tbs. honey or sugar
2   c. rolled quick cooking oats
2   c. milk
1   c. ground sunflower seeds
½   c. corn meal
½   c. oil
½   c. molasses
1½ tsp. salt
1   c. white flour
5-6 c. whole wheat flour

Follow French Bread procedure. After last rising, shape into 2 rounds, let rise and bake at 375° for 35-45 minutes, till loaf sounds hollow when tapped.

French Bread
2 loaves

Water is the trick to making that crispy crust

Soften together 10 minutes:
1 pkg. dry baking yeast
¼ c. warm-hot water
2 tsp. sugar

Add to softened yeast:
1¼ c warm water
3½ c. flour
2 tsp. salt

Use mixer to beat dough until it is too stiff for the mixer. Complete mixing by hand, pulling dough into one big mass. Turn onto floured board and knead until smooth and elastic. A finger dent pressed into dough will spring back.

Place dough in oiled bowl, turning to coat; cover and let rise till double, in warm place. Turn and push down and let rise a second time.

On lightly floured board cut dough in half. Flatten and roll up into long, thin loaves; pinch to seal. Place in French bread pans or cookie sheet, and cover with warm, damp cloth. Let rise till doubled, about 30 minutes.

Make several cuts in each loaf. Spray with water, bake at 375° for 25 minutes, until loaves sound hollow when tapped. Spray several times during baking with water, for crispiness.

Focaccia-Italian Flat Bread
8-10 rounds

1 recipe French bread
1 c. extra virgin olive oil
1 c. parmesan cheese
♥ oregano leaves, rosemary

After French bread has risen the second time, cut it into 8-10 pieces. Roll each piece into a thin ½" round and place on greased cookie sheets. Spray with water. Spread generously with olive oil, parmesan and herbs. Bake at 400° for 12-15 minutes, till golden brown.

Breads of Savory and Sweet

Onion-Walnut Rustic Loaf
1 round
If you like onions you will love this!

3 c. white flour
1 c. whole wheat flour
1 pkg. active dry yeast
2 tsp. salt
1 c. warm-hot milk
1/3 c. warm-hot water
1 c. coarsely chopped walnuts
¾ c. finely chopped onion
¼ c. soft butter
 cornmeal

Combine ½ c. flour and all of whole wheat, yeast, and salt in mixing bowl. Add milk and water and beat 2 minutes. Stir in nuts, onion and butter and beat well. Beat or knead in as much of the white flour left as to make a stiff dough. Place in oiled bowl, turning to coat all, cover and let rise in warm place till doubled.

Knead dough on lightly floured board 3-4 minutes. Shape into ball and place on cornmeal sprinkled cookie sheet. Cover, let rise 30 minutes.

Place pan of hot water in bottom of oven. Make several slashes in top of loaf. Bake at 425° for 30 minutes. Remove pan of water. Finish baking at 300° for 30 minutes.

Cheesy Quick Yeast Bread
2 loaves

1¼ c. water, warm-hot
½ c. vegetable oil
4-4½ c. flour
¼ c. sugar
2 tsp. salt
2 pkg. active dry yeast
2 eggs
3 c. grated sharp cheddar
   cheese

In bowl, combine warm-hot water, oil, 1½ c. flour, sugar, salt, yeast and eggs. Beat with mixer at medium speed for 2 minutes. Then by hand, stir in enough flour to make a stiff batter-dough and beat in cheese. Cover and let rise in warm place till doubled, about an hour.

Grease and sprinkle with cornmeal two 4"x 8" loaf pans. Beat dough down and mix-knead about 30 times. Divide in half and place in pans. Cover and let rise till doubled, 30-45 minutes.

Bake at 375°, 20 minutes, until loaf sounds hollow when tapped. Remove from pans; cool before cutting, if you can wait.

Easy Loaf
1 loaf

Basic recipe:
- $\frac{1}{4}$ c. water
- $\frac{3}{4}$ c. buttermilk
- 1 pkg. active dry yeast
- 1 Tbs. sugar
- 2 Tbs. soft butter, or oil
- $\frac{1}{2}$ tsp. salt
- $\frac{1}{2}$ tsp. baking soda
- $2\frac{1}{2}$ c. flour

Heat water and milk together to 105°-115°, warm but not too hot to the touch. Mix in a bowl with yeast and sugar and let stand for 10 minutes. Add all else and beat till smooth. Will be a soft, even sticky dough. Pat into a ball. Cover and let rise 1 hour.

Punch dough down with a floured hand and knead using a little flour, 10-20 times, to make a smooth, almost sticky, ball.

Place as a round in a greased cake pan, or as a loaf in greased bread pan. Cover and let rise 1 hour, in warm, draft-free place, until doubled. Bake at 350° for 30 minutes.

Herb bread, add:
- 1 Tbs. Italian herb mix

Onion bread, add:
- $\frac{1}{2}$ c. dry onion soup mix

Whole wheat, substitute:
- 2 c. whole wheat for 2 c. white

Whole Wheat Dinner Rolls
3 dozen

- 2 c. warm-hot milk
- $\frac{3}{4}$ c. vegetable oil
- $\frac{1}{4}$ c. honey
- 4 c. white flour
- 3-4 c. whole wheat flour
- $\frac{1}{4}$ c. sugar
- 2 tsp. salt
- 2 pkg. active dry yeast
- 2 eggs

Milk should be 120°-130°. Combine milk, 2 c. flour, 1 c. whole wheat and rest of ingredients. Beat 4 minutes at medium heat. Stir in rest of whole wheat with big wooden spoon

and enough white flour to make a stiff dough. Knead until smooth and elastic, about 5 minutes.

Place in oiled bowl, turning to oil all. Cover, let rise till doubled, 45-60 minutes. Punch down. Divide into 36 pieces and shape into balls, pulling top smooth and pinching together at bottom. Place in 9"x 12" greased baking pan and 9" square pan.

Cover, let rise in warm place till doubled- 30-45 minutes. Bake at 375° for 15-20 minutes.

Breads of Savory and Sweet

Easy Croissants
Makes 32

Easy to make, but plan for 7 hours ahead of serving. Lends itself to sweet, savory or deliciously plain

1	pkg. yeast, dry or compressed
1	c. warm water
¾	c. half and half
1/3	c. sugar
¼	c. soft butter
1	egg
5	c. flour
1	tsp. Salt
1	c. cold butter
¼	c. or more melted butter
♥	sugar, cinnamon, chopped nuts, parmesan, herbs - as you please

In bowl, soften yeast in warm water, till bubbly. Add milk, sugar, soft butter, egg, salt and one c. flour. Beat to a smooth batter.

In large bowl, cut cold butter into remaining 4 c. flour to size of peas. Pour yeast batter over this and carefully turn with rubber spatula just until all flour is moistened. Cover with plastic wrap and refrigerate at least 4 hours and up to 4 days.

Remove dough to a floured board and cut into 4 pieces. Shape pieces into smooth rounds and work with one at a time, returning the rest to the fridge.

Roll round on a floured board into a 17" diameter circle. Cut circle into 8 equal wedges. Brush with melted butter; roll up loosely from the wide end to the point end and place on ungreased baking sheet, shaping into a crescent- 1½" space between each roll. Do rest.

Cover and let rise 2 hours, until doubled in bulk. Bake at 325° for about 30 minutes, until brown.

Try cinnamon and sugar, sprinkled on before you roll them up, maybe nuts.
Or try:
spreading parmesan and a nice herb on the wedges, before rolling.

Whatever you do, it will be good.

Brioche
36 rolls

This is an elegant, fine-textured and lucious bread

Mix:
- 3 pkgs. active dry yeast
- $\frac{3}{4}$ c. warm-hot water
- 1 Tbs. sugar

In large bowl combine:
- 5 c. flour
- $\frac{1}{2}$ c. sugar
- 1 tsp. salt

In small sauce pan melt:
- $\frac{1}{2}$ c. butter

Add to butter:
- $\frac{1}{2}$ c. milk
- 4 eggs, lightly beaten

Combine all ingredients and beat 3 minutes at medium speed.
Stir in with wooden spoon (for style) $2\frac{1}{2}$ c. to $3\frac{1}{2}$ c. flour, till dough allows itself to be pulled away from sides of bowl.

Using a lightly floured surface, knead dough until smooth and elastic, about 5 minutes, using only enough flour to keep it from sticking. Finished dough will be a little sticky.

Let rise (covered and warm) till doubled, 1 hour.

Use greased muffin tins, or make 6" pie pan size or small loaf pan, or 1/3 of dough will fit a 9" cake pan. Traditional brioche is shaped as a round with a small round cap imbedded on top.

For rolls, pull pieces of dough into rounds that half fill muffin tins. Shape smaller pieces into fat, round tubes. Slash or cut top of dough in tin and stuff smaller piece into cut. Push gently closed and shape top into a knob. Same for bigger rounds.

Cover and let rise till doubled, 35-45 minutes.

Brush lightly with beaten egg and bake at 375° for 15 minutes for rolls; longer for large rounds.

Cottage Cheese Rosemary Buns
10 buns or 1 loaf

1 c. warm-hot water
2 Tbs. packed brown sugar
1 pkg. active dry yeast
4 c. flour
1 Tbs. dry rosemary
1 tsp. salt
½ tsp. pepper
1 c. small curd cottage cheese

Mix water, yeast and sugar together. Let sit 5 minutes, until foamy.

In large bowl with wooden spoon mix yeast with rest of ingredients to make a thick dough. Knead 8-10 minutes, until smooth and elastic, and finger poke pops up.

Rotate in oiled bowl to oil all. Cover and let rise in warm place till doubled, about 1 hour

Punch dough down. Turn out on lightly floured surface and cut into 10-12 equal pieces. Shape into smooth balls and flatten to about 1" thickness.

Place on greased cookie sheet, cover and let rise till doubled, about ½ hour. Bake at 400° for 15-20 minutes. Cool and split in half to use as sandwich buns.

Or roll into large rectangle and fold in thirds to place in large, greased bread pan. Let rise till doubled, 30-40 minutes and bake at 400° for 30-40 minutes till sounds hollow when tapped. Cool 10 minutes and turn out.

Boston Brown Bread

1 c. whole wheat
1 c. white flour
1 c. corn meal
¾ c. molasses
2 tsp. baking soda
½ tsp. salt
2 c. buttermilk
1 c. raisins

Grease 4 1lb. cans or 1 7" tube pan. Mix all together well and fill containers 2/3 full. Cover tightly with tin foil. Place in steamer pot on rack above boiling water.

Steam over low heat 2 hours, until firm. Only replenish with boiling water.

One Bowl Cheese Bread
1 loaf

1½ c. flour
½   c. corn meal
2   Tbs. sugar
2   tsp. baking powder
½   tsp. baking soda
1   egg
¾   c. buttermilk
¼   c. oil
1   c. shredded cheese- try jack
    with jalapeno- very yum
    Sharp cheddar is good too.

In large bowl, combine dry ingredients and cheese. Make a well in the center with bowl showing thru, and in this center place all wet ingredients. Whip wet ingredients together with a slotted spoon. Then mix with dry ingredients until just blended.

Bake in well greased 4"x 8" loaf pan for 20-25 minutes, at 375°.

Cranberry Corn Muffins
12 muffins

Whisk together:
1   c. yellow cornmeal
1   c. flour
½   c. sugar
1   tsp. baking powder
1   tsp. baking soda
½   tsp. salt

Whisk in another bowl:
2   eggs
1¼ c. plain yogurt
¼   c. butter, melted
1   c. dried cranberries

Add the flour mix to wet ingredients, and mix just until combined. Fold in cranberries.

Fill well buttered muffin tins. Bake at 375° for 20 minutes. Cool a few minutes in pan, then turn them out.

Homemade Biscuits with or without Buttermilk
10-12 biscuits

2   c. flour
3   tsp. baking powder
½   tsp. salt
¼   c. butter
¾   c. milk, or substitute:
¾   c. buttermilk for milk, and
    ½ t. baking soda for 1 t.
    baking powder

Cut butter into flour mixed with baking powder and salt, till it resembles coarse corn meal.

Add milk and mix to a smooth ball, kneading gently ½ minute. Flatten to ¾' on floured board and cut rounds.

Bake at 450° for 12-15 minutes.

Buttermilk Yeast Biscuits
2 dozen

1   pkg. active dry yeast
2   Tbs. warm-hot water
5   c. flour
¼   c. sugar
3   tsp. baking powder
1   tsp. baking soda
1   tsp. salt
1   c. butter, or vegetable
    shortening
2   c. buttermilk
♥   melted butter

Sprinkle yeast over warm water and let soften for 10 minutes, mixing a little.

Mix dry ingredients together and cut in the butter to a coarse meal texture.

Add yeast and buttermilk and mix to a smooth dough. Pat to 1" thickness on floured board and cut with 3" biscuit cutter.

Brush melted butter on top and bottom and fold in half on cookie sheet. Let rise, covered and warm, ½ hour. Bake at 400° for 20 minutes.

You can freeze them after buttering and folding in half. Pull out of the freezer when you need them. Bake at 350° for 30 minutes.

Cornbread
9 pieces

2 c. corn meal
1¼ c. flour
¼ c. sugar
2½ tsp. baking powder
½ tsp. salt
¼ c. oil
2 eggs
12/3 c. milk

Mix all dry ingredients together in bowl, using slotted spoon or whisk. Whip wet ingredients together in separate bowl. Add wet to dry and mix till just blended.

Bake in greased 9"x 9" pan for 20-25 minutes at 375°.

Corn Batter Bread
Moist and custardy-quite tasty

Beat all together:
2 eggs
6 Tbs. corn meal or flour
½ tsp. baking soda
½ tsp. salt
1½ c. buttermilk

Place 1 Tbs. butter in 1 quart baking dish or glass loaf pan and heat in oven till hot and melted. Pour batter in pan. Bake at 375° for 25-30 minutes, till set. Serve hot with butter or gravy.

Oatcakes
4 rounds

2 c. oats, pulverized in
  in blender

Add to oats:
2 Tbs. melted butter or oil
½ tsp. salt
1/3 c. hot water (you can soften the butter in the water)

Mix into a firm, smooth, not too dry paste. Cut into fourths and make flat rounds. Roll them ¼" thick and cut in wedges.

Bake at 375° for 12-15 minutes.

Good hot with butter and honey!

Irish Soda Bread
8 wedges

¾ c. raisins
2 c. flour
1 Tbs. sugar
2 tsp. baking powder
½ tsp. baking soda
1 tsp. salt
1/3 c. cold butter
1 tsp. caraway seed or
  sunflower seeds
1 egg, beaten
1 c. buttermilk or sour milk

Plump raisins in hot water and drain. Mix dry ingredients. Cut in butter till mix resembles coarse corn meal.

Make well in center of flour and add egg and buttermilk. Mix with fork just until moistened. Don't overmix.

Shape into round mound on cookie sheet, or in greased casserole dish. Bake at 400° for 20 minutes. Cut into wedges.

Indian Fry Bread
8 rounds
Can't leave the Southwest without bringing fry bread with me. Makes a great bean and/or ground turkey taco or tostada

2 c. flour
¼ c. nonfat dry milk
2 tsp. baking powder
1 tsp. salt
1 Tbs. shortening
¾ c. warm water
 cooking oil for deep fat
  frying

Mix dry ingredients together. Cut in shortening till mix resembles coarse crumbs. Mix in water. Turn out on floured board and knead till smooth.

Divide and shape into 8 balls. Cover and let rest 10 minutes. On floured surface roll each ball out to 6"-7"circle. Poke hole in the center of each and deep fry in hot oil till golden brown, one at a time.

Cover with beans, cooked taco-seasoned ground turkey, lettuce, tomato, onion, cheese, salsa.....

Maybe this should be in the main dish section. But it's good plain, too!

Sweet Breads

Streusel Coffee Cake is the treat that started me down the long road of dashing here and there with cake pans and groceries, hot ovens and too many dirty dishes; fancy decorations and colossal mess-ups, death defying deadlines, home-away-from-home at the local grocery, reading an endless stream of cookbooks like novels (I had a music teacher in college who said he could hear the music by reading the score. Now I think I know what he meant, but in taste!), finding new delectables to try out; finding what pleased my customers and what didn't, discovering I could do it and people liked my food, aching back and foots and many great adventures. I guess it was worth every anxious moment and all the hard work, like 16 hours at a shot.

This coffee cake started me down that long road because, on sudden impulse, I whipped it up– no thought, just mix, mix, bake and run– and brought it to a certain small trade fair in a certain student union just as a group of ladies trooped by. Suddenly I was surrounded and couldn't serve it fast enough! It was the smell that did it. I got the message! My endeavors were urgently needed and well appreciated! The rest is history.

Even after moving to New Mexico in 1992 I couldn't keep my nose out of cookbooks and ovens, and more adventures. So more delicious dishes have been collected along the way, their essences sprinkled here and there in this bookish endeavor. -one hundred new recipes for this new edition.

Streusel Coffee Cake

Cream together:
 1/3 c. soft butter
 ¾ c. sugar
 1 egg

Mix in:
 ½ c. milk
 1½ c. flour
 2 tsp. baking powder
 ½ tsp. salt

Streusel, mixed together:
 1 c. brown sugar, not packed
 ¼ c. flour
 1 Tbs. cinnamon
 ¼ c. butter, melted
 1 c. chopped walnuts

Spread ½ of batter in greased 9" baking pan. Sprinkle with half the streusel mix. Spread rest of batter on top and rest of streusel. Bake at 375° for 25-30 minutes, till done in middle. Of course serve hot!

Quick Sticky Buns
2 dozen

Mix in bowl and let set 10 minutes:
- 1¼ c. milk, warm-hot
- 2 pkg. active dry yeast
- 1 tsp. sugar

Add to yeast and beat with mixer for 4 minutes:
- ¼ c. soft butter
- ¼ c. sugar
- 1 tsp. salt
- 1 egg
- 2 c. flour

Add 1¼ c. flour and mix with wooden spoon to a stiff dough. Let rise in warm place, covered, till doubled and light, about 45 minutes.

Topping:
- ¾ c. butter
- 1 c. firmly packed brown sugar
- 2 tsp. cinnamon
- 2 Tbs. corn syrup
- ¾ c. chopped nuts

Melt butter in pan: add rest, mix.

Spoon scant tablespoons of topping into well buttered muffin tins, preferably deep ones.

Stir down batter and drop by full tablespoon on top of topping. Cover and let rise in warm place till pushing out of pans!

Bake at 375° for 10-15 minutes until golden. Invert onto wax paper and let sit a couple minutes upside-down. (Steams off the goodies) Lift off, and then stand back!

Popovers
8 large ones
A lazy Sunday morning treat for daughter and me, so here it is.

Place ½ tsp. butter in bottoms of 8 deep baking cups- glass are best for high popovers. Place on a cookie sheet. Heat in oven 5 minutes.

Beat together:
- 2 eggs

- 1 c. milk
- 1 c. flour
- ½ tsp. salt

Fill hot cups ½ full. Bake at 425° for 35-40 minutes, until brown and crisp. Serve right away, with butter and jam.

Biscuit Cinnamon Rolls
12 rolls
Quick and easy, a family favorite

Make one recipe of Homemade Biscuits and roll out a rectangle ½" thick. Spread or dot with soft butter and sprinkle with ½ c. brown sugar and 2 tsp. cinnamon.

Roll up like a jellyroll and slice into 12 pieces.

Melt ½ c. butter in 9" round or square baking pan. Sprinkle with 1 c. brown sugar, 1-2 tsp. cinnamon, 2 Tbs. corn syrup and maybe nuts.
Arrange slices on top of butter and sugar in pan. Bake at 425° for 15-20 minutes. Invert onto platter while hot.

Sour Cream Blueberry Muffins
12 muffins

Beat until light:
1   egg

Beat in:
½   c. sugar
2   Tbs. soft butter
1   c. sour cream

Mix together and stir in:
1 1/3 c. flour

1   tsp. baking powder
½   tsp. baking soda
½   tsp. salt

Fold in gently:
1   c. blueberries, fresh or frozen- don't thaw 'em

Bake in greased tins at 400° for 20-25 minutes.

Zucchini Bran Muffins
12 muffins

1   c. white flour
2/3 c. whole wheat flour
2/3 c. bran
½   c. brown sugar
2   tsp. baking powder
½   tsp. salt
1   tsp. cinnamon
½   c. chopped walnuts, if desired
½   c. raisins
1/3 c. vegetable oil
2   eggs

¼   c. milk
1   tsp. vanilla
3   c. grated zucchini, squeezed dry

Whisk the dry ingredients together. Whip together oil, eggs, milk and vanilla. Fold into dry ingredients with zucchini.

Bake in well buttered muffin tins at 375° for 25-30 minutes.

Oatmeal Muffins
12 muffins
Especially delicious. At the Ranch Cafe, in Taos, we served these Texas style (big!) with lots of blueberries. With or without, they are great.

Soak together for 1 hour:
- 1   c. quick cooking oats
- 1   c. buttermilk, or sour milk

Cream together:
- 1/3 c. soft butter
- ½   c. packed brown sugar
- 1   egg

Stir into the creamed mixture with the oats and milk:
- 1   c. flour

- 1   tsp. baking powder
- ½   tsp. baking soda
- ½   tsp. salt

Fill greased muffin tins 2/3 full and bake at 375° for 20-25 minutes.

For blueberry variation, fold in:
- 1½ c. blueberries mixed with
- ¼ c. flour

"Filled Doughnut " Muffins
10-12 muffins

Fine textured and satisfies the doughnut urge

Cream together well:
- 1/3 c. soft butter
- ½   c. sugar
- 1   egg
- 1   tsp. vanilla

Mix together and stir in:
- 1¼ c. flour
- 1½ tsp. baking powder
- ½   tsp. salt
- ¼   tsp. nutmeg

With:
- ½   c. milk

Fill greased muffin tins 1/3 full. Indent middle and fill with scant teaspoon your favorite jelly. Add more batter over top, filling tin 2/3 full. Press down around sides. Bake at 350° for 20 minutes.

Immediately roll hot muffins in:
- 6   Tbs. hot melted butter

Then roll them in a mixture of:
- ½   c. sugar
- 1   cinnamon, if desired

Serve hot.

Banana-Orange Muffins
12 muffins

2 bananas
2/3 c. orange juice
☺ zest, 1 orange
1 egg
6 Tbs. butter, melted, cooled
2 c. flour
½ c. sugar
1 tsp. baking powder
1 tsp. baking soda
½ tsp. salt

Mash bananas in mixing bowl. Whisk in orange juice, zest, egg and butter.

Mix dry ingredients together. Blend into wet ingredients.

Bake in greased muffin tin at 400° for 15 minutes, until done in middle.

Variation: Can also add ½ cup chopped dates and ½ cup chopped nuts.

Old World Pastry Crisps
36 little tasties

2 c. flour
1 c. butter
1 egg, separated
¾ c. sour cream

Topping:
¾ c. sugar
¾ c. finely chopped pecans
1 tsp. cinnamon

Cut butter into flour with pastry blender and then with fingers to blend it more. Mix in egg yolk and sour cream, to make a smooth dough. Shape into a cylinder, wrap in plastic and chill several hours.

Cut roll into 3 parts, working with one at a time. Roll out on a lightly floured board, a circle about 1/8" to ¼" thick. Sprinkle with 1/3 of sugar mixture. Cut into 12 wedges. Roll up each wedge, starting at the wide end.

Brush with egg white and sprinkle with sugar.

Place on greased cookie sheet, and bake at 375° for 25-30 minutes, until brown. While still warm, loosen from cookie sheet so they don't stick when cool. Cool, if you have the will power to wait.

Blueberry Buckle Coffee Cake

Mix together in large bowl:
- 2 c. flour
- ¾ c. sugar
- 2 tsp. baking powder
- ½ tsp. baking soda
- ½ tsp. salt

Whip together and fold into dry mix:
- ¾ c. buttermilk
- ¼ c butter, melted
- 1 egg
- 1 tsp. vanilla
- 1-2 tsp. grated lemon or orange peel

Batter will be stiff so towards end, fold in:
- 2 c. blueberries, frozen or fresh

Spread in greased 9" square baking pan. Sprinkle with topping: Mix together:
- ½ c. sugar
- 1/3 c. flour
- ¼ c. soft butter
- 1 tsp. cinnamon

Bake at 350° about 55 minutes, until done in middle.

Coconut Coffee Cake

Cream together:
- 1/3 c. soft butter
- ½ c. sugar

Beat in:
- 4 egg yolks
- ½ tsp. almond extract

Mix together:
- 1 c. flour
- 1½ tsp. baking powder
- ¼ tsp. salt

Mix dry ingredients into butter mix alternately with:
- ½ c. milk

(half dry, all milk, half dry)

Smooth into well greased 9"x9" baking pan.

Topping:
Beat till almost stiff:
- 4 egg whites

Beat in till stiff:
- 1 c. sugar

Fold in:
- 1 c. flaked coconut
- ½ tsp. almond extract

Spread carefully over batter in pan.

Sprinkle over top:
- ½ c. chopped almonds or coconut, or both

Bake at 325° for 30 minutes, until done in middle.

There won't be enough left to serve any way but warm.

Rhubarb Coffee Cake

Beat until smooth:
- 1½ c. brown sugar, firmly packed
- 1 c. buttermilk
- 2/3 c. oil
- 1 Tbs. vanilla
- 1 egg

Add and mix well:
- 2½ c. flour
- 1 tsp. baking soda
- ½ tsp. salt

Stir in:
- 2 c. chopped rhubarb, fresh or frozen

Pour into 9"x 9" greased baking pan.

Top with:
- ½ c. sugar
- 1 Tbs. butter, rubbed together

with fingers till crumbly.

Bake at 325° for 50-60 minutes, until toothpick stuck in middle comes out clean.

Maple Walnut Coffee Cake

For crumb mix, mix well:
- 1½ c. flour
- 1 c. finely chopped walnuts
- 2/3 c. firmly packed brown sugar
- 6 Tbs. soft butter
- ½ c. pure maple syrup

Mix together and set aside:
- 2 c. flour
- 1½ tsp. baking powder
- ½ tsp. baking soda
- 1 tsp. salt

Cream together:
- ½ c. soft butter
- 2/3 c. firmly packed brown sugar
- 1/3 c. pure maple syrup
- 1½ tsp. maple extract
- ½ tsp. vanilla

Beat in:
- 2 large eggs
- ¾ c. sour cream

Mix in the flour mixture

Butter and flour a 9" springform pan. Fill with ½ the batter; then half the crumb mix, then half the batter and finish with crumb mix.

Bake at 350° for 50-60 minutes, until toothpick in the middle comes out clean. Cool for 5 minutes and remove sides of pan.

Transfer to plate and serve.

Almond Bread

Cream all together:
- 1 c. blanched ground almonds (can use blender)
- 1/3 c. chopped almonds, toasted
- ½ c. soft butter
- ½ c. sugar
- 2 Tbs. cream

- 2 tsp. vanilla
- 1 tsp. almond extract
- 2 eggs
- ¾ c. flour
- ½ tsp. baking powder

Bake in greased and floured loaf pan at 325° for 45-50 minutes. Cool completely before cutting.

Date Nut Bread

- ½ lb. dates (1½ c.) pitted and chopped
- 2 c. boiling water
- 1½ c. sugar
- ½ c. soft butter
- 2 eggs
- 4 c. flour
- ½ tsp. salt
- 2 tsp. baking powder
- 1 c. chopped nuts

Pour boiling water over dates and set aside.

Cream butter and sugar. Beat in eggs. Add rest, including dates, and beat until smooth and glossy

Bake in 2 greased loaf pans, 325°, 1 hour, until toothpick comes out clean. Serve with cream cheese.

Soft Applesauce Bread

Pour ¾ c. hot water over 1 c. instant oatmeal. Set aside.

Cream together:
- 1 c. sugar
- 1 c. brown sugar
- 2 eggs
- 1 c. vegetable oil
- 1 tsp. vanilla
- ¾ c. unsweetened applesauce

Mix together and add to creamed mixture:
- 1½ c. flour
- 1 tsp. allspice
- 1 tsp. cinnamon
- 1 tsp. baking soda
- ½ tsp. salt

Add oatmeal and mix.

Bake in 2 medium greased loaf pans, at 350°, for 35-40 minutes. Or try several small baby loaf pans for nice presents.

Applesauce Gumdrop Holiday Loaf

3   c. flour
2   c. sugar
½   tsp. baking powder
1½   tsp. baking soda
1   tsp. salt
1   tsp. cinnamon
½   tsp. nutmeg
½   tsp. cloves
½   tsp. mace or allspice
½   c. soft butter
1/3 c. buttermilk
2   eggs, beaten
1½   c. unsweetened applesauce
2½   c. fruit flavored gumdrops
     cut smaller, if large ones

1   c. chopped walnuts
1   c. golden raisins

Mix dry ingredients together.
Beat in butter, milk and eggs.
Fold in applesauce with gumdrops,
walnuts and raisins.

Bake in 2 greased bread pans at
350°, 35-45 minutes, or till done
in the middle. When cool, ice with
Powdered Sugar Icing and decorate
with gumdrop slices.

Banana Loaf

This is Grandma's never fail banana bread. Can add nuts, but it's great
without

Cream together well with mixer:
2   c. sliced bananas (2 or 3)
¼   c. soft butter
½   c. sugar (or maple syrup)

Add:
2   c. flour
2   tsp. baking powder

½   tsp. baking soda
½   tsp. salt
½   c. sour milk or buttermilk,
     whipped with:
2   eggs

Bake in greased loaf pan at 350°
for about 45 minutes.

Pumpkin Bread

1   16 oz. can pumpkin puree
2   c. sugar
2/3 c. soft butter
½   c. buttermilk
3   eggs
2½   c. flour
2   tsp. baking soda
1   tsp. salt

2   tsp. cinnamon
½   tsp. cloves

In mixing bowl, beat first 5
ingredients. Add rest and beat till
smooth. Bake in greased loaf pan
at 350° for 50-60 minutes, till
done in the middle.

Blender Pancakes
12 cakes
These are thin, tender, and full of protein

1	c. cottage cheese
6	eggs
½	c. flour
¼	c. oil
5	Tbs. milk
½	tsp. vanilla

Mix all in blender together and bake on lightly greased griddle, ¼ c. for each cake. Serve with butter and syrup. Try current jelly, like Swedish pancakes.

Raised Waffles
5- 9" waffles
Very light with a crispy outside.

1	pkg. active dry yeast
¼	c. warm-hot water
1¾	c. warm milk
¼	c. soft butter
2	Tbs. sugar
½	tsp. salt
2	c. flour
3	eggs

In large bowl dissolve yeast in warm-hot water and wait 10 minutes till it bubbles. Add rest of ingredients and beat till smooth. Cover and let rise in the fridge overnight. Bake on greased, hot waffle iron.

Also good with half whole wheat flour.

Sour Cream Waffles
8 waffles

Good with whipped cream and fruit

3	eggs, separated
¾	c. milk
¾	c. sour cream
½	c. butter, melted
1½	c. flour
2	tsp. baking powder
½	tsp. baking soda
1	Tbs. sugar

Whip the egg whites stiff and set aside.

Beat egg yolks with milk, sour cream and butter. Mix in dry ingredients. Carefully fold in egg whites.

Bake in a hot waffle iron. Serve with you-know-what. Try folding in 1 c. blueberries before baking.

Russian Pancakes (Sirniki)
20-24 pancakes

2 eggs, separated
4 oz. soft cream cheese
1 Tbs. sugar
½ tsp. salt
1 c. small curd cottage cheese
½ c. flour
4 Tbs. butter
℮ sour cream and jam

Whip egg yolks, cream cheese, sugar and salt together. Blend in cottage cheese and flour well.

With clean beaters, whip egg whites until stiff. Fold into cheese mix.

Using a large non-stick skillet, drop by well-rounded spoonful onto lightly buttered surface, keeping them well apart. Lightly brown on one side and turn.

Keep warm while doing rest, and serve.

Blueberry Buckwheat Pancakes
15- 4" pancakes

½ c. buckwheat flour
½ c. flour
2 tsp. baking powder
2 tsp. sugar
½ tsp. salt
1 c. milk
2 eggs
¼ c. oil
1½ c. blueberries, fresh or frozen

Mix dry ingredients together.

Whisk milk, eggs and oil together. Mix into flours, blending well.

Bake on hot, oiled griddle, 1-2 minutes each side. Serve hot with butter and maple syrup.

Cookies

Grandma's Santa Cookies

When I was a little girl, every Christmas I could expect under the Christmas tree, from my Grandma Mimi, a box of chocolate covered cherries, a small gift, and a tin of cookies,

These cookies were rather special- made of Lebkuchen and cut out as Santas. From somewhere she found and adorned them with bright colored paper-stick-on-Santa-heads.

I would gobble them nonchalantly , enjoying them with the innocence children have. I mean, they came every Christmas, didn't they? And that was good, wasn't it?

But now- even many years later- when I am quiet and think about it, I find those Grandma Santa Cookies still there, in the soft, tender part of my heart, like a candle in the window, lighting the way. (Thank-you, Grandma. I don't know if I ever even thanked you.)

Lebkuchen
4-5 dozen
Traditionally, these are baked several weeks in advance and stored airtight to mellow the flavors.

½ c. honey
½ c. molasses
¾ c. packed brown sugar
1 egg
1 tsp. grated lemon peel
1 Tbs. fresh lemon juice
2¾ c. flour
½ tsp. baking soda
1 tsp. allspice
1 tsp. cloves
1 tsp. nutmeg
1 tsp. cinnamon

Mix honey and molasses in saucepan and heat to just boiling. Cool completely. Beat in brown sugar, egg, lemon peel and juice. Mix in remaining ingredients.

Cover and refrigerate at least 8 hours.

Roll out small amount of dough at a time on floured board. Keep rest of dough in fridge. Cut into rectangles, 2½" x 1½", or cut into different shapes.

Bake 1" apart on greased cookie sheets, at 400°, 10-12 minutes, till no indent remains when poked.

Brush with glaze while still warm. Loosen and cool. Store airtight.

Glaze:
Mix until smooth:
1 c. powdered sugar
1 Tbs. warm water
1 tsp. light corn syrup
Add more water, if needed, a drop at a time to get it spreadableness.

Russian Tea Cakes
3-4 dozen

Cream together:
1 c. soft butter
½ c. powdered sugar
2 tsp. vanilla

Mix in:
2¼ c. flour
¼ tsp. salt
¾ c. finely chopped nuts

Roll into 1" balls and bake on ungreased cookie sheet at 375° for 10-12 minutes until set and barely brown. While warm, roll in powdered sugar. Cool and roll in powdered sugar once again.

Greek Powdered Sugar Butter Cookies
3 dozen

1   c. butter
½   c. powdered sugar
1   egg yolk
3   Tbs. brandy and 1 tsp.
    vanilla, or
2   Tbs. cream and 1 Tbs.
    vanilla
2   to 2½ c. flour
½   c. blanched almonds,
    toasted and chopped fine

Cream butter with mixer in bowl for 15 minutes, till light colored and fluffy. Gradually add ½ c. powdered sugar and beat 5 minutes. Beat in egg and flavoring with 2 c. flour. Add almonds and enough flour to make a soft dough that doesn't stick to the sides of the bowl.

Shape walnut size pieces into crescents and bake 1" apart on ungreased cookie sheet at 350° for 20 minutes, until golden. Loosen and cool for 5 minutes.

Sprinkle 1 c. powdered sugar on a sheet of wax paper. Transfer hot cookies to sheet, placing them close together. Pile powdered sugar liberally all over them. Cool and unbury them to serve.

Such a ritual! They've gotta be good after all that!

Snickerdoodles
4 dozen

An old reliable with a twist

1½   c. sugar
1   c. butter
2   eggs
2¾   c. flour
2   tsp. cream of tartar
1   tsp. baking soda
¼   tsp. salt

Cream butter, sugar and eggs together. Mix in rest.

Shape into 1½" balls. Roll in a mixture of:
¼   c. sugar
1   Tbs. cinnamon
½   tsp. ground cardamom

Bake 2" apart on ungreased sheet at 400° for 10 minutes, until the centers are almost set. Loosen and cool on rack.

Thumbprints
1½- 2 dozen

Cream together:
- ½ c. soft butter
- ¼ c. packed brown sugar
- 1 egg yolk

Stir in:
- 1 c. flour
- ¼ tsp. salt

Roll into 1" balls and dip in:
- 1 egg white, slightly beaten

Roll in:
- ¾-1 c. finely crushed walnuts

Place 1" apart on ungreased cookie sheet. Bake 5 minutes at 375° and remove from oven. Working quickly, make indent in top of cookie with thumb and place ½ tsp. red jelly or jam in indent. Return to oven for another 8 minutes. Cool on rack.

Scotch Shortbread
2 dozen

So simple and so sublime!

- 1 c. soft butter
- ½ c sugar
- 2¼ c. flour

Mix well with hands. Pat evenly into 9" square pan. Poke with fork every ½". Bake at 325° for 20-25 minutes till lightly brown. Cut while warm 4x6.

Nutmeg Buttons
3½ dozen

Cream together well:
- 1 c. soft butter
- ¾ c. sugar
- 2 tsp. vanilla
- 2 tsp. rum or orange extract
- 1 egg
- 1½ tsp. nutmeg

Add and mix well:
- 2½ c. flour

Using palms of hands, roll into walnut size pieces and flatten slightly. Bake on ungreased cookie sheets at 350°, 12-15 minutes, till lightly brown. Frost with rum frosting and sprinkle with nutmeg.

Rum Frosting
Cream together well:
- 2½ c. powdered sugar
- ½ c. soft butter
- 2-3 Tbs. milk or cream
- 1 tsp. rum extract
- 1 tsp. vanilla

Chewy Shortbread Chocolate Chip Cookies
2½ dozen

¾ c. butter
½ c. sugar
¾ c. packed brown sugar

1¾ c. flour
1 tsp. baking soda
½ tsp. salt
1 tsp. vanilla

6 oz. chocolate chips
1 c. chopped nuts

Cream butter and sugars. Mix in rest. Roll into walnut size balls and flatten slightly on cookie sheet. Bake at 375° for 12 minutes, until set.

Choco-Chip Oatmeal or Raisin Cinnamon
3-4 dozen

This was a popular trade fair treat.

Mix together well:
1 c. soft butter
1 c. sugar   2 eggs
1 c. packed brown sugar
1 tsp. baking powder
1 tsp. baking soda
½ tsp. salt
1 tsp. vanilla
1½ c. quick cooking oats
2 c. flour

Add:
1 12 oz. pkg. chocolate chips
¾ c. chopped nuts

Form into 1-2" balls. Dip in sugar and bake on ungreased cookie sheets sugar side up, at 375° for 10-12 minutes.

Oatmeal raisin: Omit chocolate chip and add 1-2 tsp. cinnamon and 1 c. raisins.

Chocolate-chocolate: Add 1 more cup oats and pulverize all oats in blender. Add 4 oz. melted semi-sweet baking chocolate to cookie dough with the chocolate chips and nuts.

Chinese Almond Cookies
3-4 dozen

1¼ c. sugar
1 c. soft butter
2 c. plus 2 Tbs. flour
1 tsp. almond extract
3 egg yolks
1 c. chopped almonds
1 tsp. baking soda

☺ toasted almond half, garnish

Cream all together well. Form into walnut size balls. Press almond half on top. Bake at 300° for 20 minutes on ungreased cookie sheets. Loosen and cool.

Fruit Filled Softies
5 dozen

2 c. packed brown sugar
1 c. soft butter
2 eggs
½ c. buttermilk
1 tsp. vanilla
3½ c. flour
1 tsp. salt
1 tsp. baking soda
¼ tsp. cinnamon

Cream sugar and butter. Mix in rest of ingredients. Drop by teaspoonful 2" apart on ungreased cookie sheet. Place a small teaspoon filling on top of each cookie. Top with a small teaspoon of dough, spreading it a bit.

Bake at 400° for 10-12 minutes. Cool on rack.

Date filling: Cook 2 c. small cut dates, ¾ c. sugar and ¾ c. water over low heat, stirring constantly, until thickened. Can add ½ c. chopped nuts.

Apricot-Cherry Filling: Cook 1½ c. minced dried apricots, 1 c. sugar, ½ c. fine chopped maraschino cherries, and ¾ c. water over low heat, stirring constantly, until thickened.

Try your own combinations.

Almond Tiles
2½ dozen
Delicate and crisp

2 c. flour
¾ c. soft butter
¼ c. sugar
1 tsp. almond extract
1 egg, separated
1 c. almonds, blanched and sliced
☺ sugar

Mix flour, butter, sugar, extract and egg yolk together well with hands. Will start out dry and come together as you mix. If too dry, add up to 1 Tbs. water while kneading.

Roll out half of dough at a time on lightly floured board to a rectangle 9"x 10". With pastry brush, brush dough with half the egg white. Sprinkle with half the almonds and 1 Tbs. sugar. Cut dough 3 x 5, into 3"x 2" rectangle.

Bake at 375° on ungreased cookie sheet for 10-12 minutes.

Vanilla-Orange Crisps
5 dozen

1	c. sugar	
1	c. soft butter	
1	egg	
2	tsp. vanilla	
2	c. flour	
2	tbs. grated orange peel	
½	tsp. baking soda	
½	tsp. cream of tartar	

Mix well and chill at least an hour.

Roll dough into 1" balls and place 2" apart on ungreased cookie sheet. Flatten with bottom of glass dipped in sugar. Bake at 375° for 8-10 minutes, until light brown and middle is just set.

Jumbo Gingersnaps
10 big ones

½	c. sugar	
2¼	c. flour	
¾	c. vegetable oil	
¼	c. molasses	
¼	c. maple syrup	
2	tsp. baking soda	
1	tsp. ground ginger	
½	t. cinnamon	
½	tsp. ground cardamom	
¼	tsp. salt	
1	egg	
☺	extra sugar	

Mix all but extra sugar together well. Pour ½ c. sugar in a wide bowl. Shape ¼ c. dough into a ball and roll in the sugar, coating all over evenly. Dough will be soft.

Bake 3" apart on ungreased cookie sheet at 350° for 15 minutes. Cool cookies on a rack.

Almond Freezer Cookies
4 dozen

Beat until fluffy:
- 1 c. soft butter
- 1 c. sugar

Add and mix well:
- 1 Tbs. almond extract

Stir into stiff dough:
- 2¼ c. flour
- ♥ pinch salt

Halve dough and roll into 2" logs. Wrap in plastic wrap and freeze several hours. Slice thick or thin ¼" to ½" for crispy or chewy cookies. Bake 375° for 10-12 minutes on lightly greased cookie sheet. Remove right away and cool. Can ice and decorate.

Rocky Road Thumbprints
2 dozen

½ c. packed brown sugar
½ c. soft butter
3 Tbs. unsweetened baking cocoa
½ tsp. vanilla
1 egg
1 c. flour
¼ tsp. salt
1 c. marshmallow cream
½ c. toasted chopped almonds

Cream all together well. Shape by tablespoons into balls. Place 3" apart on ungreased cookie sheet. Press thumb deeply into center of each.

Bake at 350° 8-10 minutes, until firm. Cool on rack. Place 1 tsp. marshmallow cream in centers and sprinkle with almonds.

Holiday variation: Substitute ½ cup crushed peppermint candy cane for almonds.

Coconut Slices
6 dozen

Especially tasty flavor.

1 c. soft butter
1 c. sugar
1 egg
½ tsp. almond extract
1 c. flaked coconut
2¼ c. flour
½ tsp. baking soda
♥ toasted almond halves

Cream butter and sugar together. Beat in eggs and almond extract. Stir in coconut and dry ingredients and mix well to a solid mass.

Roll into three 8" logs. Wrap well and freeze 3 hours or more. Each roll makes about 2 dozen slices, 3-4 slices per inch. Place 2" apart on ungreased cookie sheet.

Mix together:
1 egg yolk
1 Tbs. milk

Brush slices with egg yolk mix and top with toasted almond halves or coconut. Bake at 325° for 15-20 minutes, till light brown.

Vienna Tarts
24 tarts
A luscious treat from my child hood; my mother's specialty.

½ c. small curd cottage cheese
½ c. soft butter
1 c. flour
❦ raspberry jam, or other tart
  jam of choice
  (but raspberry is the best)

Cream butter. Blend in cottage cheese and flour to make a smooth dough. Form into a flattened rectangle and chill for an hour. Roll dough into a 13"x 19" rectangle and trim to even the sides, making rectangle 12"x 18". Cut into two dozen 3" squares, (4x6).

Place a scant teaspoon of jam in the center of the square- not too much so it seals properly.

Have a cup of water on hand and, using the tip of a finger, moisten the edges and fold over to make a triangle, allowing the bottom edge to stick out more than the top edges. Now fold the bottom edge up over the top edge and pinch together to seal well- to avoid hot jam spill.

Place tarts on cookie sheet and bake at 400° for 10-12 minutes, until tarts are light brown and jam bubbles a bit.

Different way:
Center each square of pastry in a tart pan or muffin tin hollow. Place 1 tsp. of jam in center and pinch the four corners of pastry together over the jam. Bake.

English Tea Cakes
3 dozen
These rise like a drop cookie and cool with a succulent, dry crumb.

½ c. soft butter
¾ c. sugar
1 egg, separated
3 Tbs. milk
1¾ c. flour
1½ tsp. baking powder
¼ tsp. salt
1 tsp. vanilla
♥ sugar

Mix all ingredients together thoroughly, leaving out egg white. Chill a couple hours, covered. Roll into walnut size balls. Dip tops, first in egg white, then in sugar.

Place sugar side up on ungreased sheet, 2" apart and bake at 350° for 12 minutes, till light brown.

Filled Cookies
3 dozen

First time I made these was for a dance in high school. Good then and good now.

Cream together:
- ½ c. soft butter
- 1 c. sugar

Beat in:
- 2 eggs
- 2 Tbs. whipping cream
- 1 tsp. vanilla
- 2½ c. flour
- ¼ tsp. baking soda
- ½ tsp. salt

Chill dough. Roll thin, 1/8", and cut into 3" rounds. Place on greased cookie sheets.

Fill with 1 full teaspoon of fruit filling, on one side of the round. Fold over and pinch closed. Bake at 350° for 8 minutes till very light brown, no more, to avoid being too dry.

Fruit Filling:
- 1½ c. finely minced dried fruit, such as dates, figs, raisins, apricots
- ½ c. sugar
- ½ c. water
- 2 tsp. fresh lemon juice

Cook over low heat, stirring constantly till thick, about 5 minutes. Cool.

Try with chocolate covered mints instead of fruit filling.

Molasses Ginger Crisps
4 dozen
Crisp and flavorful. Made without white sugar or eggs

Heat to boiling:
- 1 c. molasses

Stir in:
- ½ c. soft butter
- 1 tsp. baking soda

Mix in well:
- 2¼ c. flour
- 1¾ tsp. baking powder
- ½ tsp. salt
- 1½ tsp. ground ginger

Chill dough. Either roll out very thin and cut into desired shapes, or shape a ball of dough into a thin tortilla with fingers.

Bake on lightly greased cookie sheet at 350°, 5-7 minutes. Don't overbake. Loosen and cool.

Old World Filbert Cookies
3-3 ½ dozen sandwich cookies

Especially tasty for a party

1   c. butter
½   c. sugar
2   c. flour
1   Tbs. cream
¼   tsp. salt
1½ c. finely ground hazelnuts
❦ currant jelly

Cream butter and sugar and cream. Mix in flour and salt. Divide into 2 parts and shape into rolls 1¾" wide.

Wrap well and freeze for several hours. Slice thicker than 1/8" and thinner than ¼" (3/16"). Bake on ungreased sheets at 350° for 8-10 minutes, until light brown.

Loosen and cool. Sandwich 2 cookies with jelly and frost with White Icing.

White Icing: Beat together till smooth: 2 c. powdered sugar and 3 Tbs. milk.

Stuffed Snowballs
2 dozen

Dough:
Cream together:
½   c. soft butter
¾   c. powdered sugar
1   Tbs. vanilla

Work in by hand
1½ c. flour
♥ pinch salt

Stuffing:
♥ your choice of maraschino cherries, chocolate kisses, almonds, cashews....

Shape a tablespoon of dough around goody of your choice to form a ball. Bake on ungreased cookie sheet at 350° for 12-15 minutes. Cool. Spread with glaze and decorate with chopped nuts, coconut, etc., if desired, before icing sets.

Glaze:
Beat until smooth:
1   c. powdered sugar
1½ Tbs. milk
1   tsp. vanilla

Almond-Ginger Crisps
5 dozen

1 c. almonds, blanched, chopped fine
1¼ c. flour
½ c. sugar
½ c. soft butter
1/3 c. dark corn syrup
1 tsp. ginger
1 tsp. cinnamon
¾ tsp. cloves
½ tsp. salt

Reserve ¼ cup almonds for the tops of cookies. Mix rest of ingredients together well.

Roll out dough 1/3 at a time on lightly floured board, ¼" thick. Cut out cookies with 2" round scalloped cutter. Press a few almonds on top. Bake on greased cookie sheet, 1" apart, at 350° for 10 minutes.

Applesauce Raisin Cookies
4 dozen

½ c. soft butter
1 c. sugar
½ c. brown sugar
1 egg
1 c. applesauce
1¾ c. flour
1 tsp. baking soda
½ tsp. baking powder
½ tsp. salt
1 tsp. cinnamon
½ tsp. cloves
½ tsp. nutmeg
1 c. quick cooking oats

1 c. raisins
1 c. chopped nuts, if desire

Cream together butter and sugars. Beat in applesauce and egg. Stir in dry ingredients with raisins and nuts.

Drop by large teaspoon onto greased cookie sheet. Bake at 375° about 15 minutes.

A soft, tasty cookie, decorative in a little kid's hand.

Banana-Nut Rounds
4 dozen

Chewy and flavorful!

2 1/3 c. flour
1 c. sugar
1 c. soft butter
½ c. banana slices
¼ tsp. salt
1 tsp. vanilla
½ c. chopped pecans

Cream all together well. Shape into 1" round balls and place on greased cookie sheet 2" apart. Flatten to ¼" thick with sugared bottom of glass. Bake at 375°, 12-15 minutes till edges are light brown. Remove immediately. Sandwich 2 cookies with your favorite frosting, if desired.

Almond or Cashew Butter Cookies
3½-4 dozen

½ c. soft butter
½ c. sugar
½ c. firmly packed brown sugar
2/3 c. almond or cashew butter
1 egg
1 tsp. almond or vanilla extract
1¾ c. flour
1 tsp. baking soda

½ tsp. salt
☺ sugar for topping

Cream butter and sugar together well. Beat in rest. Roll into apricot size balls. Dip in sugar. Place sugar side up on ungreased sheet and criss-cross with fork to flatten. Bake at 350° for 12-15 minutes till set.

The Best Chocolate Cookies Ever
3 dozen

1 c. soft butter
1 c. firm packed brown sugar
1 c. sugar
¾ c. unsweetened baking cocoa
2 eggs
2 tsp. vanilla
2½ c. flour
1 tsp. baking soda

¾ c. nuts, if desired

Cream all together well. Roll into walnut size pieces and dip one side into sugar. Place sugar side up on ungreased cookie sheet. Bake at 375°, 5-7 minutes till set and slightly cracked.

Lemon Crisps
2½ dozen

21/8 c. flour
¾   tsp. baking powder
¼   tsp. salt
1   c. soft butter
1   c. sugar
2   egg yolks
2   tsp. fresh lemon juice
☺   grated peel of 1 lemon

Cream butter till shiny and smooth. Add sugar, cream well.

Beat in egg yolks and remaining ingredients. Shape into large walnut size and place on lightly greased cookie sheets.

Using flat bottom of 3" glass or jar lid (on jar), dip in sugar and flatten cookies, dipping in sugar once more when half flattened, to about 1/8" thick. Bake at 350° for 10 minutes, till edges are delicately browned.

Teatime Tassies
2 dozen

3   oz. soft cream cheese
½   c. soft butter
1   c. flour

¾   c. packed brown sugar
1   Tbs. soft butter
1   egg
2   tsp. vanilla
2/3 c. coarsely chopped pecans
1-2 tsp. orange zest, if desired

To make pastry, blend cream cheese, butter and flour. Chill an hour.

Shape into 24 1" balls. Place each ball in ungreased 1¾" (tiny) muffin tins and press onto bottom and up sides, making a hollowed out shell.

Bring the sides up a little higher than the surface of muffin tin to prevent spilling over while baking.

Beat together brown sugar, 1 Tbs. butter, egg, zest and vanilla. Divide ½ the pecans among pastry cups and fill with egg-sugar mix. Top with rest of pecans. Bake 325°, 25 minutes.

Also good using ½ pecans and ½ chocolate chips.

White Chocolate Macadamia Nut Cookies
4 dozen

Cream till fluffy:
- 1 c. butter
- 1 c. sugar
- ½ c. firmly packed brown sugar
- 2 tsp. vanilla
- 2 eggs

Add the following and blend well
- 2 c. flour
- 1 tsp. baking soda
- 1 tsp. salt
- 6 oz. white chocolate candy bars or chips, or vanilla bark, chopped into pieces
- 1 c. macadamia nuts, chopped in smaller pieces to spread the flavor. Use more if you don't mind the price.

Place 2" apart on ungreased cookie sheets and bake at 350° about 15 minutes, until light brown.

Chocolate! Substitute 6 oz. chocolate chunks instead of white, or do both!

Delicate Tea Wafers
4½ dozen
An impressive, refined party sandwich cookie

- 1 c. soft butter
- 1/3 c. whipping cream
- 2 c. flour
- ♥ sugar
- ♥ Butter Icing from Full Hearts recipe

Mix butter, cream and flour together well. Cover and chill several hours.

Roll out 1/3 of dough at a time, keeping rest chilled. Roll 1/8" thick on floured board and cut into 1½" circles

With spatula, transfer to wax paper thickly layered with sugar. Pat and turn to coat both sides well.

Place on ungreased sheet and prick with fork 4 times. Bake 7-9 minutes at 375° till just set but not brown. Loosen and cool.

Sandwich with butter icing or other of your choice.

Full Hearts
25-30 double cookies

Such a nice valentine cookie!

Cream together:
- ½ c. plus 1 Tbs. soft butter
- 1 c. sugar
- ½ tsp. orange extract
- 1 tsp. vanilla

Beat in:
- 1 egg

Stir in:
- 11/3 c. flour
- ¼ tsp. baking soda
- ¾ tsp. baking powder
- ♥ pinch salt

Stir in:
- 1/3 c. sour cream
- ♥ powdered sugar

Roll out on lightly floured board to 3/16" thick. Cut dough out with a 2" or 3" heart shape cutter Cut out the middle of half of them with a smaller size heart shape, removing the center piece, creating a window.

Bake at 350° on an ungreased cookie sheet for 10 minutes, until lightly brown. The center pieces can also be baked, or tossed back into the dough supply.

Top cookie: When cool, gently sift powdered sugar over the window pieces to evenly coat them with a gentle blanket of white.

Butter Icing: Beat together
- 2 c. powdered sugar,
- 2 Tbs. soft butter,
- 2½ Tbs. cream
- ½ tsp. vanilla.

Frost the bottom whole heart shape evenly and to edges with butter icing. Position "window" heart on top, pressing together gently. (You can sift powdered sugar over top now, if desired, or touch up, anyhow.) Allow them to harden for ½ hour.

Fill window center with:
- ♥ raspberry jam
Using tip of spoon, place scant teaspoon of jam in window. Using bottom of same spoon spread jam gently to fill the window.

What beauties!

Coconut Macaroons
2 dozen

2 egg whites, room temp
¾ c. sugar
4 tsp. potato or rice flour
2 c. coconut flakes

Beat egg whites foamy and beat in sugar till sugar is dissolved. Fold in flour and coconut.

Shape into walnut size pieces and place on greased cookie sheet. Flatten to ¼" thickness with bottom of glass- dipped in sugar to keep from sticking. Bake at 325° for 20 minutes, till light brown.

Try: Substitute for coconut:
   1 c. ground almonds
   1 c. fine chopped dried fruit, like apricots or cherries

Try: Sandwich two macs with jam or favorite frosting.

Lace Cookies
4 dozen
These graced many a fancy catering table and gala party

2/3 c. packed brown sugar
½ c. light corn syrup
½ c. butter
1 c. flour
1 c. finely chopped nuts
☺ sweetened whipped cream

Heat at medium temperature, brown sugar, corn syrup and butter to just boiling, stirring constantly. Remove from heat and stir in flour and nuts. Keep batter warm over hot water.

Drop by teaspoon 3" apart on lightly greased cookie sheet- 8 cookies (rows of 2, 1 ,2, 1, 2) Bake at 375° till set, about 5 minutes. Don't let them turn dark. Cool a few minutes- just long enough that they hold shape - and loosen carefully with a spatula. If any stick, remove the loose ones to a level surface and return the sheet to the oven for a few moments until the cookie unsticks. Eat as is, or:

While the cookies are warm and pliable they can be shaped. Wrap them around a clothes pin or dowling to make a tube. Or use a cream horn mold to make a cornucopia shape. Or press gently into a muffin tin hollow to make a basket with wavy sides.

Work fast before they harden, tho you can reheat them briefly to resoften them. Fill them with sweetened whip cream. Try a few berries for garnish.

Greek Honey Cakes
2 dozen

Very unusual and absolutely sweetly delicious.

- 1 c. soft butter
- ¼ c. powdered sugar
- ¼ c. orange juice or 2 Tbs. concentrate plus 2 Tbs. water
- 2 tsp. grated orange rind
- 1 tsp. baking powder
- 1 tsp. cinnamon
- ¾ tsp. cloves
- 2½ c. flour
- 1 c. ground walnuts

Cream butter in bowl till light and fluffy, 5 minutes. Beat in all but walnuts to make a soft dough. Chill an hour in fridge.

To form cookies, shape a large walnut size to a round.

Then roll to slightly elongate, like a fat tube. Then flatten slightly, to make a flat oval.

Bake on ungreased cookie sheet 1" apart at 325° for 20-25 minutes. Immediately drop hot cookies in hot syrup and leave until syrup is well absorbed. Remove with slotted spoon and place on serving dish. Sprinkle with nuts while still sticky.

Syrup: In large saucepan, boil over medium heat for 10 minutes:
- 1 c. sugar
- 1 c. water
- ½ c. honey
- 1 Tbs. fresh lemon juice
- ½ orange or lemon

Delicate Butter Wafers with Chocolate Glaze
4 dozen

- 1 c. soft butter
- 2/3 c. sugar
- 2 tsp. vanilla
- 1 egg
- 2½ c. flour
- ¾ tsp. baking powder

Cream butter smooth and shiny. Beat in sugar thoroughly. Beat in eggs and vanilla till fluffy. Mix in flour and baking powder. Cover and chill 1 hour.

Keeping rest chilled, roll out 1/3 of the dough to a 1/8" thickness on lightly floured board. Cut 2" circles and set 2" apart on ungreased cookie sheet. Bake at 425° for 4-5 minutes, to delicate brown.

Glaze: Melt a generous cup of chocolate chips with 2 Tbs. butter. Using thin spatula, swirl onto cookies, covering thinly.

Oatmeal Fudge-Nut Brownies
24 biggies

From Mark Rosen, who wanted Fairfield to have this recipe.

Cream together till light:
- 1   c. soft butter
- 2   c. brown sugar
- 2   eggs
- 1   Tbs. vanilla

Add following and mix well:
- 2½   c. flour
- 1   tsp. baking soda
- 1   tsp. salt
- 3   c. quick cooking oats
- 1½   c. coarse chopped walnuts

Press 2/3 of mix into 9" or 10"x14" greased pan.

Filling: Melt together over low heat, blending constantly:
- 1   12 oz. pkg. chocolate chips
- 1   15 oz. can sweetened condensed milk
- 3   Tbs. butter
- 1   tsp. vanilla

Spread filling over brownie mix in pan. Sprinkle and spread rest of brownie mix over top. Bake at 350° for 20-25 minutes. Cool and cut 4x6.

Watch out! At the Ranch Cafe in Taos, we called these "Psycho Bars."

Quick Buttermilk Brownies
12-16 pieces

Cream together well, to dissolve sugar:
- 2/3   c. oil
- 2   c. sugar
- 2   tsp. vanilla
- ½   c. buttermilk
- 2   eggs
- 2   c. flour
- ¾   c. unsweetened baking cocoa
- 1   tsp. baking soda
- ½   tsp. salt

Bake in greased and floured 9"x 12" pan at 350° for 25 minutes, until just set in the middle and crispy on edges.

Cool and frost with Chocolate Glaze.

Chocolate Glaze: Melt together over medium heat, mixing to a smooth paste:
- ¼ c. butter
- 1/3 c. milk
- 2/3 c. unsweetened baking cocoa

Beat in, to a glossy smoothness:
- 3 c. powdered sugar
- 1 tsp. vanilla

Spread while warm. Cool and cut.

White Chocolate-Raspberry Brownies
16-24 bars

½ c. butter
2 c. (12 oz.) vanilla chips or baking bar, coarse chopped
2 eggs
½ c. sugar
1 tsp. vanilla
1 c. flour
½ tsp. salt
¾ c. raspberry jam
¼ c. sliced almonds, toasted

Melt butter. Remove from heat and add 1 c. of the vanilla pieces. Let stand without stirring.

In large bowl, beat eggs light and foamy. Beat in vanilla and sugar till lemon colored. Stir in melted chips, then flour and salt, until just mixed.

Spread half of batter in greased and floured 9" square baking pan. Bake at 325° for 15-20 minutes, till light brown. Mix rest of chips in rest of batter and set aside in fridge.

Place jam on hot crust and allow to soften a few minutes, then spread evenly. Taking teaspoons of the remaining cold batter, flatten them gently with fingers and cover top of jam. (Jam will show thru, but crust melts fast enough to spread) Sprinkle almonds on top.

Bake at 325° another 25-30 minutes till center is done. Score top while still warm but not hot. Cool and cut the scoring into bars.

Almond Jam Bars
24 regular, 32 tea size

Good example of simple being sublime. Many happy customers, like Suzy M.

Cream together:
¾ c. soft butter
½ c. powdered sugar
1 tsp. almond extract

Mix in till crumbly and a touch clumpy:
1¾ c. flour
½ c. fine chopped almonds

Reserve scant 1 c. of mixture for topping and press rest firmly into 9"x 12" baking pan.

Spread over crumb layer:
1 12 oz. jar (1½ c.) apricot or raspberry jam

Mix reserved topping with
½ c. slivered or sliced almonds

Crumble over top of jam in small clumps. Bake at 350° till golden, 30-35 minutes. Cut while warm, 4x6 or 4x8.

Lemon Bars
24 pieces

Cream with fingers (or mixer) till mixture clings together:
- 1½ c. flour
- ¾ c. powdered sugar
- ½ c. butter, soft

Pat into 9"x 12" baking pan and bake 10-12 minutes at 350°, till light brown.

Beat together 5 minutes:
- 5 eggs
- 1¼ c. sugar
- 2 Tbs. grated lemon peel

Add and beat smooth:
- 10 Tbs. fresh lemon juice
- 1/3 c. flour
- ½ tsp. baking powder

Pour onto cookie base. Bake at 350° for 20-25 minutes until light brown and just set. Cool.

Sift powdered sugar over top. (Can use a mesh strainer for this, with a small amount of sugar and tapping the sides.) Cut 4 x 6 pieces and touch up powdered sugar before removing from pan.

Pecan Pie Bars
24 pieces

Crust:
- 1¾ c. flour
- ½ c. soft butter
- ¼ c. brown sugar

Cream together and pat evenly into 9"x 12" baking pan. Bake 10 minutes at 350°.

Cream together:
- 1 c. light corn syrup
- 1 c. packed brown sugar
- 5 eggs
- 2 c. chopped pecans
- 1 tsp. vanilla
- ¼ c. butter, melted

Pour over crust and bake 25-30 minutes, 350°, till set in middle.

Butterscotch Bars
24 pieces

- ½ c. butter
- 2 c. brown sugar
- 2 eggs
- 1 Tbs. vanilla
- 1 c. flour
- 2 tsp. baking powder
- 1 c. chopped nuts, if desired

Melt butter in saucepan; beat in rest. Bake in greased 9"x 12" pan at 350° 20-25 minutes. Cool and frost with Powdered Sugar Icing Glaze (page 189). Cut 4x6. They won't be happy with anything less. Another e.g. of "so simple and so sublime"!

Date Bars
24 of 'em

Cream together well:
- ¾ c. soft butter
- 1 c. brown sugar

Stir in and mix well:
- 1¾ c. flour
- ½ tsp. baking soda
- ½ tsp. salt
- 1½ c. quick cooking oats

Pat half of crumb mix in 9"x 13" greased baking pan. Bake 10 minutes at 350°.

Date Filling: Mix together in saucepan and cook 10 minutes over low heat, stirring constantly:
- 3 c. cut up dates
- ¼ c. sugar
- 1½ c. water

Spread cooled date mix over baked crust, and cover with remaining crumb mixture. Bake at 375°, 25 minutes. Cool & cut.

Malted Milk Bars
36 bars

- 2 c. flour
- 1 c. sugar
- ½ c. packed brown sugar
- 3 tsp. baking powder
- ½ tsp. salt
- ¾ c. soft butter
- 1 egg
- ¾ c. chopped nuts, if desired

Place all but nuts in large bowl and mix at low speed till crumbly; stir in nuts. Press all but 1 c. of mixture in bottom of 9"x 12" ungreased pan.

Combine all together:
- 2 c. powdered sugar
- 8 oz. pkg. soft cream cheese
- ½ c. malted milk
- ¼ c. soft butter
- ¼ c. unsweetened baking cocoa
- ¼ c. milk
- 1 egg
- 1 tsp. vanilla

Pour over crumb crust. Sprinkle rest of crumb mix evenly over top. Bake at 350° for 40 minutes, until golden. Chill, cut in bars, 6x6.

Heath Bars
2-3 dozen

Mix together:
- 1 c. flour
- ½ c. firm packed brown sugar
- ½ c. soft butter

Pat into ungreased 9"x 12" pan. Bake at 350° for 8-10 minutes. Cool slightly.

Blend well:
- 1 c. packed brown sugar
- 2 Tbs. flour
- 1 tsp. baking powder
- 2 eggs
- 6 oz. chocolate chips
- ½ c. chopped nuts, if desired

Spread over baked crust. Bake for 15 minutes or so, until golden brown and set in middle.

Remove from oven and immediately sprinkle over top:
- 6 oz. chocolate chips

Wait 5 minutes, till chips are soft, and spread quickly with a spatula. Cool and cut.

Better Than Fruitcake Bars
24 bars

Cream together:
- 1 c. flour
- ¾ c. packed brown sugar
- ½ c. soft butter
- 1 egg
- 2 tsp. grated orange or lemon peel
- ½ tsp. baking soda
- ½ tsp. cinnamon
- ¼ tsp. salt

Mix together:
- 1½ c. maraschino halves
- 1 c. dried apricots, cut in sixth's
- 1 c. coarse cut dates
- 1 c. coarse chopped pecans
- ¼ c. flour

Mix fruit into creamed mixture. Spread in greased and floured 9"x 12" baking pan. (Fingers are good for this one.) Bake at 350° for 25 minutes. Cool completely.

Make glaze and drizzle over top.

Glaze:
- 1/3 c. sugar
- 3 Tbs. orange juice concentrate

Heat in small pot over medium heat, stirring constantly, until slightly thick.

Cut 3x8.

Cashew-Pecan Bars

2 dozen

A different, tasty bar, well worth the caramelizing process, which really isn't so hard.

Caramel:
1	c. sugar
2	Tbs. water
2	Tbs. cream
2	Tbs. light corn syrup
2	Tbs. butter

1	c. chopped pecans
¾	c. flour
¾	c. quick cooking oats
2/3	c. packed brown sugar
½	tsp. baking soda
½	tsp. salt
1	egg
1/3	c. soft butter
1	jar (7 oz.) marshmallow creme
1½	c. roasted, salted cashew pieces or halves

For caramel, mix sugar and water in a heavy-bottomed saucepan. Mix over medium-high heat till sugar is dissolved, then turn on high.

Cook without stirring, but you can swirl, until sugar turns an even amber color. Remove from heat and add cream, syrup and butter, whisking to smoothness. Watch for splatters.
Set aside while making base.

Mix dry ingredients together with pecans and egg. Cut in butter with a fork, till crumbly. Press into ungreased 9"x 12" baking pan. Bake at 350° for 10 minutes.

Spoon marshmallow creme over hot crust and spread evenly. Drizzle with caramel. Sprinkle with cashews.

Bake about 15 minutes, until set. Cool before cutting, 6x4, using wet knife.

Cakes

Confessions of a prolific cake baker

Things aren't always all roses. I do confess that sometimes I fall back on my Russian cabbage heritage. I confess, I often used the same bowl for making several cakes in a row, without washing it, starting with white and ending with chocolate. The bright side is: I scraped the bowl very clean with my rubber spatula. So there's roses there , too. I won't tell you what I did with the beaters.

I confess that I am sure, even when I retire from this job (soon!), there will be days when I suddenly spring up out of nowhere and head for the kitchen and whip together a cake in a few minutes flat. And then, since we won't be eating much sugar (bad for you), I'll probably give most of it to a neighbor or stranger who comes to the door or lurks around. Once that sugar, butter, flour and vanilla is in your veins, it's hard to let go! Besides, it's a creative process!
(It happened)

I confess to an impressive statistic: One Friday I baked two 16" layers (4 recipes) vanilla cake, two 10" layers plus two 6" layers (2 recipes) vanilla cake, one 12"x18" spice cake (2 recipes), one 12"x18" poppy seed (using only egg whites), one 12"x18" (2 recipes), lemon–orange (using the egg yolks), two 9" layers chocolate (2 recipes), and two 10" layers garbanzo-spice cakes(I washed out the bowl for that one 'cuz he was allergic to wheat), and then frosting and decorating them all, all from 1:00 p.m. to 4:30 p.m.– $3\frac{1}{2}$ hours. I also cooked for the Trade Fair that day, as well.

My poor mixers! They didn't last very long mixing all those cakes in those great big bowls: right hand holding that poor, little cheapie electric mixer whizzing away, while the left hand scraped the sides with the rubber spatula and turned the bowl , all at the same time.

But a big hobart wouldn't fit in my kitchen and those fancy stand mixers were too awkward and not quick enuf for my frenzied pace, or the size of the recipes. Besides , it was cheaper buying a bunch of little ones than one big one even tho they did keep burning out.

I did finally break down and buy a more expensive hand held, and I have it to this day. Probably cus it stays in the drawer a lot more. And I finally did get rid of all those extra beaters

I confess to back and bone-breaking endurance stints that I never thought I could do, but did. (And I'm paying for now)

I confess to things I haven't confessed and probably won't.
AndI confess to never getting tired of all the sounds of appreciation and rave reviews.
I was needed! Many thanks to you!

Tids and Bits and other Items of Interest

- ♥ Always do your baking- pies, bread, cookies, cake.-in a preheated oven.
- ♥ Bake in the middle of the oven, away from the sides, for more even cooking
- ♥ If ever a cookie sticks to the sheet before you can loosen it, back to the oven for a minute to resoften and un stick!
- ♥ None of the recipes call for sifted flour. With my measuring cup I toss the flour up a bit to lighten it. Then I scoop up my cup of flour, or whatever, and level it with a knife, or, after many hundreds of cups, give it a flick of the wrist and the top tumbles to a perfect levelness, more or less
- ♥ Oil does not make a good greaser (expect for potatoes) as the pan still sticks. Butter, margarine, shortening, are the answer.
- ♥ For a recipe that calls for buttermilk, you can substitute sour milk. Make sour milk by adding 2 Tbs. of vinegar to a cup of milk.
- ♥ To whip whipping cream, first chill beaters and bowl in the freezer. Sit the bowl on top of a bag of frozen veggies while whipping the cream. Keeps everything chilled and whippable, especially in hot weather when you don't have air conditioning.
- ♥ Garbanzo (Besan) flour is the best substitute I have found for wheat flour. Smells wierd raw, but bakes up perfectly and looses the smell..
- ♥ Use the same amount as regular white flour. Trust me! It works!

Basic White Cake

The mixing and baking procedure used in this cake is a standard for many of the others. Therefore, it is first on the list as a reference for the others that follow. Not all the cakes follow this procedure, and those types have their own directions. But this is the basic way I whip up most of my cakes. I come back to this procedure over and over because the cakes come out great, with half the trouble- helpful for a busy schedule!

Place in a large mixing bowl:

- 2¾ c. flour
- 1¼ c. sugar
- ¾ c. soft butter or margarine
- 2 tsp. vanilla, or other extract of your choice
- 3 tsp. baking powder
- ½ tsp. salt

Measure out:

- 1¼ c. milk

Add 2/3 of the milk, about, to ingredients in bowl. Beat for 2 minutes.

(Mix at low speed till flour is mixed enough not to fly, then up the speed and beat for 2 minutes. This completely incorporates the butter and dissolves the sugar and makes a thick batter. If you add all the liquid at once it is too thin to cream the butter.)

Add with the rest of the milk and beat 2 minutes:

- 3 eggs

(Beat at high speed. Adding the eggs at the last helps keep the batter smooth. It will look curdled at first and then magically transform into a harmonious creaminess.)

Grease and flour your baking pans, either two 9" rounds or one 9"x12" rectangle, or one 12" round. Tap the flour around the greased pan, covering it all. Then turn it upside-down over sink and rap sharply on edge of sink to knock out the loose stuff.

Bake at 350° for 25-30 minutes for 9" rounds, or 35-40 minutes for larger pan, or until center is solid (doesn't poke down or leave a depression, but rather feels spongy when lightly touched with a finger. Or toothpick comes out clean when poked in the center).

Cool a few minutes in pan, loosen all around with a thin blade, and invert on cooling racks. Fill and frost when completely cool.

Eggless White Cake

3 c. flour
1¾ c. sugar
2/3 c. soft butter or margarine
2 tsp. vanilla
3 tsp. baking powder
1½ tsp. baking soda
1¾ c. buttermilk

See Basic White Cake recipe for mixing and baking directions.

Silver Cake

22/3 c. flour
1¾ c. sugar
¾ c. soft butter or margarine
2 tsp. vanilla
4½ tsp. baking powder
½ tsp. salt
1¼ c. milk
5 egg whites

See Basic White Cake recipe for mixing and baking directions.

Chocolate Cake

2 c. flour
12/3 c. sugar
1 c. soft butter or margarine
1 tsp. vanilla
1 c. unsweetened baking cocoa
1½ tsp. baking powder
1 tsp. baking soda
½ tsp. salt
11/3 c. water
3 eggs (or 2/3 c. buttermilk for an eggless cake)

See Basic White Cake recipe for mixing and baking directions.

I haven't added any frosting/filling suggestions, thinking everyone had their own ideas about that and there are plenty to choose from later on in the chapter.

Moist Brown Sugar Cake

2 2/3 c. flour
1¾ c. packed brown sugar
¾ c. soft butter
or margarine
1 tsp. vanilla
3 tsp. baking powder
1 tsp. baking soda
½ tsp. salt
1 1/3 c. buttermilk
3 eggs

See Basic White Cake Recipe for mixing and baking instructions

Exotic Spice Cake

2 c. cake flour, or 1 7/8 c. all-purpose flour
1 2/3 c. sugar
¾ c. soft butter or margarine
3 Tbs. unsweetened baking cocoa
1 tsp. vanilla
1 tsp. orange extract
1 tsp. almond extract
½ tsp. baking powder
½ tsp. baking soda
1 cinnamon
½ tsp. nutmeg
½ tsp. allspice
½ tsp. salt
¾ c. buttermilk
3 eggs

See Basic White Cake recipe for instructions, adding all spices with butter.

Spice Cake

2¾ c. flour
1 c. sugar
1¼ c. brown sugar, not packed
¾ c. soft butter or margarine
1½ tsp. baking soda
1½ tsp. cinnamon
1 tsp. nutmeg
1 tsp. allspice
½ tsp. ground cloves
½ tsp. salt
1 c. buttermilk
3 eggs

See Basic White Cake recipe for directions, adding all spices with butter.

Carrot Cake

2 c. plus 2 Tbs. flour
2 c. sugar
1 c. vegetable oil
2 tsp. baking powder
1 tsp. baking soda
2 tsp. cinnamon
½ tsp. salt
4 eggs

Beat all together till smooth, 2 minutes.
Beat in :
3 c. grated carrots

See Basic White Cake for baking instructions. Frost with Cream Cheese Frosting. Can add 1 c. drained, crushed pineapple and 1 c. nuts, if desired.

Banana Cake

2½ c. flour
1½ c. sugar
2/3 c. soft butter or margarine
1¼ c. bananas, packed in (about 3 bananas)
1¼ tsp. baking powder
1¼ tsp. baking soda
½ tsp. salt
2/3 c. buttermilk
2 eggs

Follow Basic White Cake recipe for instructions, creaming bananas with butter

Applesauce Cake

2½ c. flour
2 c. sugar
½ c. soft butter or margarine
1½ tsp. baking powder
½ tsp. baking soda
1 tsp. cinnamon
½ tsp. allspice
½ tsp. ground cloves
½ tsp. salt
1½ c. unsweetened applesauce (use as milk in recipe)
1/3 c. apple juice (use as milk)
2 eggs (or 1/3 c. buttermilk)

See Basic White Cake recipe for instructions.

Orange Juice Cake

Use the Lemonade Cake recipe and substitute grated peel of large orange and 6 oz. orange juice concentrate for lemon peel and lemonade.

Moist Brown Sugar Chocolate Cake

2½ c. cake flour, or 2 c. plus 6 Tbs. all-purpose flour
1¾ c. packed brown sugar
¾ c. soft butter or margarine
3 1 oz. squares unsweetened baking, melted, cooled
2 tsp. vanilla
½ tsp. salt
2½ tsp. baking powder
1½ c. milk
1 whole egg plus 3 egg yolks

See Basic White Cake recipe for instructions. Cream in the chocolate with the butter.

Poppy Seed Cake

Use White or Orange or Lemonade Cake recipe, and add ¼ c. poppy seeds. Lemon Frosting is good with this.

Lemonade Cake

2 2/3 c. flour
1½ c. sugar
2/3 c. soft butter
♥ grated peel of 2 lemons
1½ tsp. baking powder
1 tsp. baking soda
½ tsp. salt
1 6 oz. can lemonade, plus enough buttermilk to make 1 1/3 c. liquid
3 eggs

See Basic White Cake recipe.

Maple Syrup Cake

Low in white sugar!

Mix together:
2¼ c. cake flour
½   c. sugar
½   c. soft butter or margarine
3   tsp. baking powder
1   tsp. maple extract
½   tsp. salt

Mix together:
1   c. maple syrup
½   c. milk

Pour two-thirds of maple/milk into flour mix and beat 2 minutes.

Add rest of liquid with
2   eggs
½   c. toasted nuts, if desired

Beat batter for 2 minutes. Bake in two 8" round pans at 350° for 20-25 minutes. Frost with whipped cream sweetened with maple syrup.

Secret Ingredient Chocolate Cake

Mix in a large bowl:
2   c. flour
1½   c. sugar
1/3 c. unsweetened baking cocoa
2   tsp. baking soda

Add and mix with mixer for 2 minutes:
1   c. mayonnaise
1   c. warm water
1   tsp. vanilla

Bake in two greased and floured cake pans at 350° for 30 minutes. Cool. Frost with Coffee Frosting.

Coffee Frosting
Cream all together, starting at low speed:
1   c. soft butter
1¾   c. powdered sugar
3-4 Tbs. strong, warm coffee
2   Tbs. unsweetened cocoa

Blend at high speed after incorporating the sugar. Fill middle and frost top and sides.

Yes, the secret ingredient was mayonnaise. Did you take the dare? And wasn't it one of the best cakes ever?

Chocolate Mousse Cake

1   recipe Chocolate Cake
1   recipe Chocolate Mousse
    Cream
1   recipe Chocolate Glaze

Split cooled cakes with serrated knife, slipping a flat plate under the top half to lift it off. Fill 3 layers with Mousse Cream and top with last layer. Chill while making Chocolate Glaze.

When glaze is at spreading consistency, frost from top to bottom. Glaze will be semi-fluid while you spread it, but cools to a solid. If it gets too cool, heat moments on stove, stirring, to make it spreadable again.

Decorate with chocolate curls. Barely warm a thick chocolate bar (no nuts), and shave with a potato peeler. They curl up and look cute.

Black Forest Deluxe

1   Chocolate Cake recipe,
    your choice which
3   c. whipping cream, whipped
    with 6 Tbs. sugar
1   21 oz. can prepared cherry
    pie filling
1   recipe Dark Cherry Topping

Bake cake in two 9" cake pans. Fill between layers with the cherry pie filling. Spread 1/3 of whipped cream on top of the cherries.

Frost stacked sides with remaining cream. Using a spatula or piping tube build up an edge around top of the cake.

Fill in top with following topping:

Dark Cherry Topping:
1   16 oz. can dark, sweet
    cherries (save juice)
1   c. drained cherry juice plus
    fresh lemon juice, to fill in
4   tsp. cornstarch
2   Tbs. sugar

Mix all but cherries in saucepan and cook, stirring constantly, till thickened. Stir in cherries and cool completely

Spread on top of cake; chill and serve.

Whip Cream Cake

1½ c. whipping cream,
     whipped stiff
3 eggs
1½ c. sugar
1 Tbs. vanilla
2 c. flour
2 tsp. baking powder
½ tsp. salt

Beat together eggs, sugar and vanilla until light, about 2 minutes. Fold in with spatula the dry ingredients to whipped cream, mixing smooth.

Bake in two, 9" pans. Good frosted with Chocolate Mousse Cream, Raspberry Cream, Lemon Icing, strawberries and cream, or...,or...

Fancy Walnut Cake

Using above recipe, fold ¾ c. walnuts (smashed with rolling pin) into batter, and bake.

Split cake (horizontally, of course) while still a little warm, and spread raspberry or apricot jam between the splits. Put halves back together and fill and frost the cakes with Cream Cheese Icing.

Spread jam on top forming a circle or heart shape. Outline jam with piped icing or fresh fruit.

Splitting the cake isn't as hard as it may seem. A long, serrated knife works best. Even if it's crooked, no one will pay attention, except to gawk and make many compliments to the chef!

Queen of Almond Cake

1 recipe White or Silver
   Cake recipe
1 recipe French Silk Butter
   Frosting I or II, or White
   Chocolate Buttercream
1½ to 2 10 oz. cans almond
   filling (like Solo)
¼ c. sliced toasted almonds

Bake in two 9" round pans. Cool cake; have frosting ready

Split each layer in half with serrated knife. Carefully spread half of almond filling on the bottom half of each split cake, then replace top half.

Fill and frost cakes. Sprinkle almonds over top.

Rich and Moist Buttermilk Cake

Separate :
  5   large eggs, room temp

With clean beaters and bowl, beat the egg whites to soft peaks
Gradually beat in, tablespoon at a time:
  ½ c. sugar, until stiff peaks are formed

Cream together in separate bowl:
  1½ c. sugar
  1   c. butter
  2   tsp. vanilla
  1   tsp. baking soda
  ½ tsp. salt

Beat in one at a time the 5 egg yolks.

Mix into batter:
  2   c. plus 2 Tbs. flour
  1   c. buttermilk

Fold egg whites into batter. Bake at 325° in two 9" round cake pans, greased and floured, for about 35-45 minutes, till done in middle.

Fill with Custard Filling, frost with French Butter Silk, and topped with jam or nuts.

Coconut Cake

  1   recipe Buttermilk Cake
  2   recipes Custard Filling

Fold into custard:
  2 c. flaked coconut

Frosting:
  2 c. whipping cream
  ¼ c. sugar
Whipped together to firm, soft peaks

Topping:
  2   c. coconut flakes

Split baked layers, making 4 layers. Fill with coconut custard to make 3 layers of filling as you pile each split layer on top of the next. Cover with whipped cream and pat coconut all around, covering cake completely. Chill.

Italian Supreme

  1   recipe Whipped Cream Cake or Buttermilk Cake
  1   recipe Ricotta Filling
  1   recipe White Chocolate Buttercream or Whipped Cream

☺ jam of your choice

Split cake and fill middles with favorite jam. And fill middle of cakes with ricotta filling. Frost with your choice frosting.

Oatmeal Cake with Caramelized Apples
Extra special different and delicious.

4	Granny Smith apples, peeled, cored, ¼ inch slices
2/3	c. sugar
1/3	c. water
3	Tbs. soft butter
1	c. quick oats
1½	c. boiling water
½	c. butter, soft
1	c. white sugar
1	c. brown sugar, not packed
2	eggs
1½	c. flour
2	tsp. cinnamon
1	tsp. baking soda
1	tsp. vanilla
½	salt
½	c. chopped walnuts

Dissolve sugar and water in large saucepan, and cook over high heat, without stirring, until sugar turns golden, about 3-5 minutes.

Stir in the apples and cook until they are soft, 5-6 minutes, stirring to coat evenly as they cook. Spread the 3 Tbs. butter thickly over bottom of glass 9"x12" baking dish and thinly up the sides. Arrange apples evenly over bottom.

Mix oats and boiling water and let stand 1 hour. Cream butter and sugars and beat in eggs. Add rest of ingredients, including oats, and mix well. Spread over apples and bake at 325° for 40 minutes, or until center is dry.

Loosen sides and turn up side down onto platter immediately. Let sit there a few minutes to steam fruit out of pan. Might have to coax a few of the apples down. Serve hot or cold. Try sweetened whipped cream or ice cream.

Toasted Pecan Cake

Use any of the vanilla cake recipes and fold into batter ¾ c. of toasted, chopped pecans.
(Toast at 325° for 5-7 minutes in oven, till brown.)

Frost with Mocha, Penuche, French Silk or Cream Cheese Frosting. To go really all out, fold into the frosting 1 c. toasted, chopped pecans. So tasty!

Orange Walnut Cake
10" tube cake

3 eggs
1 c. butter, melted and cooled
1 c. sugar
2 Tbs. grated orange peel
2 c. flour
2 tsp. baking powder
1 c. chopped walnuts
1 c. plain yogurt

Beat eggs until light and yellow color. Add butter, sugar and orange rind, mixing well. Beat in flour and baking powder. Fold in yogurt and walnuts.

Pour into greased and floured 10" tube pan and bake at 350° for 40-50 minutes-without opening oven for the first 40 minutes.

Cool for 5 minutes and spoon cooled syrup over cake and let set for 2-3 hours. Remove from pan and place on platter.

Ice with Powdered Sugar Icing Glaze, using orange juice, and stud with:
$\frac{1}{2}$ c. toasted slivered or sliced almonds

Syrup:
$\frac{1}{2}$ c. sugar
$\frac{1}{2}$ c. orange juice concentrate
$\frac{1}{2}$ c. water or orange liqueur
Mix and bring to a slow boil in saucepan, stirring occasionally, until sugar is dissolved, 5 minutes. Cool.

Christi's Rhubarb Cake

$\frac{1}{2}$ c. soft butter or margarine
2 c. sugar
1 egg
1 tsp. vanilla
1 c. buttermilk
$\frac{1}{2}$ tsp. salt
1 tsp. baking soda
$2\frac{1}{2}$ c. flour
4 c. chopped rhubarb
$\frac{1}{2}$ c. chopped walnuts

Cream butter and $1\frac{1}{2}$ c. sugar. Add buttermilk, egg, vanilla, salt and baking soda. Blend in flour. Stir in rhubarb.

Spread in a greased and floured 9"x 12" baking pan, preferably non-metal. Sprinkle top with nuts and $\frac{1}{2}$ c. sugar. Bake at 350° for 35-45 minutes, until center is done. Pour glaze over warm cake.

Creamy Butter Glaze
Mix in saucepan and boil 4 minutes:
$\frac{1}{2}$ c. butter
$\frac{3}{4}$ c. sugar
$\frac{3}{4}$ c. evaporated milk or half & half
1 tsp. vanilla

Mexican Chocolate Torte

1 c. whole almonds, toasted and cooled
1/3 c. firmly packed light brown sugar
1 Tbs. cinnamon
½ tsp. salt
5 ounces bittersweet chocolate, chopped
5 eggs, separated
1 tsp. vanilla
1/3 c. sugar

Easy Chocolate Glaze:
4 ounces bittersweet chocolate, chopped
2 Tbs. butter
2 Tbs. heavy cream
1 Tbs. light corn syrup

Icing:
¼ c. powdered sugar
1 tsp. milk, about

Butter an 8" or 9" spring form pan. Line the bottom with a round of wax paper and butter it. Dust the pan with flour.

In a food processor or blender add almonds, sugar, cinnamon, salt and blend till almonds are fine ground. Add chocolate and process it fine. (might get a little pasty in blender- no problem) Turn out into bowl and beat in egg yolks and vanilla.

In separate bowl, whip egg whites with pinch salt to soft peaks and beat in the sugar gradually till meringue just holds stiff peaks. Whisk a third into the chocolate to loosen it and fold in the rest completely.

Pour batter into pan, smooth top and bake at 325° for 45-55 minutes. Cool on rack for 5 minutes, run a knife around the edge of cake and remove the rim. Cool completely and remove bottom.

For glaze, set metal bowl over barely simmering water and add all glaze ingredients. Stir until melted and smooth; cool till lukewarm.

Put rack with cake on top of a piece of wax paper. Pour glaze over torte and drizzle down sides. Let set.

Mix milk with powdered sugar a little at time to bring it to dripping consistency but not too thin. Drizzle a decorative pattern on cake top.

Ginger Pound Cake

¾ c. soft butter
8 oz. soft cream cheese
1½ c. sugar
1½ tsp. vanilla
4 eggs
1¾ c. flour
1½ tsp. baking powder
¼ c. minced candied ginger
♥ grated peel of 1 lemon or orange

Cream butter and cream cheese till and fluffy. Beat in sugar and vanilla. Mix in rest. Bake in greased and floured large bread pan at 350° for 60-70 minutes, until done in middle. Cool in pan. Loosen and turn out.

Almond-Filled Bundt

Glaze;
1 c. sugar
½ c. water
1 tsp. each: vanilla, almond, rum and lemon extracts

Boil sugar and water together for 5 minutes. Stir in extracts after cooling a little.

Cake:
1½ c. soft butter
2 c. sugar
5 eggs
1 tsp. each: vanilla, almond, rum and lemon extracts
3½ c. flour
1 tsp. baking powder
1 c. milk

Cream butter and sugar light and fluffy. Beat eggs and extracts in well. Fold in dry ingredients with milk. Spread 2/3 of batter in greased and floured bundt or angel food cake pan.

Filling:
1 12 oz. can almond filling
1 8 oz. can almond paste

Mix filling and paste to a smooth creaminess. Spread carefully on top of batter, staying 1" away from outside and inside edges. Carefully spread rest of batter on top.

Bake at 350° for about one hour or a little more, till center of cake is solid. After cooling cake in pan 5 minutes, pour cooled glaze evenly over top. Let cake cool in pan. Loosen and remove to cooling rack.

Icing:
1 recipe Powdered Sugar Icing Glaze
½ c. toasted, chopped almonds

Spread glaze on cake and decorate with nuts. Let drip and then remove to serving platter.

Sherry Pound Cake

1½ c. soft butter
3 c. packed brown sugar
5 eggs, separated
1 Tbs. vanilla
3½ c. flour
1½ tsp. baking powder
½ tsp. nutmeg
½ c. milk
½ c. cream sherry
¼ c. white sugar

Cream butter in large bowl until creamy. Beat in sugar until well creamed. Beat in egg yolks and vanilla.

Combine dry ingredients together. Combine milk and sherry. (Don't worry about the curdled look.) Mix dry ingredients alternately with wet just until smooth.

With clean beaters, whip egg whites till almost stiff and gradually add ¼ c. sugar, beating to glossy stiffness. Fold into batter.

Bake in greased and floured 10" bundt pan at 325° for 1 hour and 10-20 minutes. Cool 10 minutes in pan and turn out on rack to cool completely.

Lemon Cream Cheese Bundt Cake

1¼ c. sugar
½ c. soft butter
1 8 oz. pkg. soft cream cheese
3 eggs
2¼ c. flour
3 Tbs. grated lemon peel
3 tsp. baking powder
½ tsp. salt
1 c. milk

Combine first four ingredients at low speed and then blend at high speed for 3 minutes. Add rest, beating just till blended.

Bake in 10" tube pan, greased, even if non-stick, at 350° (325° if it has colored exterior), for 45-55 minutes, until toothpick stuck in center comes out clean. Cool in pan 20 minutes, then invert onto platter. Brush all over with glaze and cool.

Glaze: Combine:
1/3 c. sugar
¼ c. lemon juice

Fruit Up-Side-Down Cake

What gorgeous splendor and taste! Why settle for plain pineapple in orderly show! Let overflowing cornucopia prevail, to celebrate the fruits of the world!

1¼ c. flour
2/3 c. sugar
1½ tsp. baking powder
½ tsp. salt
1/3 c. soft butter
½ c. milk
1 tsp. vanilla
2 eggs
1/3 c. butter
½ c. packed brown sugar
1 16 oz. can apricots, drained
1 8 oz. can chunked pineapple, drained
1 generous c. dark sweet cherries, fresh or frozen (or try figs, mandarin oranges, raspberries, blackberries... you get it.)

Place first 5 ingredients in mixing bowl. Add milk and vanilla and cream till smooth, 2 minutes.

Add eggs and beat smooth, 2 minutes. Heat 9" square glass baking pan in oven with 1/3 c. butter in the bottom, till butter is melted. Sprinkle brown sugar over melted butter.

Arrange 2 overlapping apricot halves in 9 even spaces, cut side up, so they will be centered on cake pieces cut 3x3. Arrange pineapple and cherries around them. Pour batter over all and bake at 350° for 40-50 minutes, until center is solid.

Because this cake is so juicy in it's underpinnings, the center might still be soft while the top is baked over. If this happens, slit the center open to let the steam escape, to bake the middle faster.

Place large plate on top of baked cake and turn up-side-down to position fruit on top. Let sit a minute for juices to settle and remove pan. Great served warm.

Three Layer Chocolate Cake with Cream Cheese Chocolate Frosting

Outstanding, intense chocolate on all levels

1 c. unsweetened baking cocoa
4 oz. unsweetened baking chocolate
2 c. boiling water
1¼ c. soft butter
2¾ c. sugar
4 eggs
2 tsp. vanilla extract
2¾ c. flour
2 tsp. baking soda
½ tsp. baking powder
½ tsp. salt

Whisk cocoa, chocolate and water together in bowl. Set aside to cool a little.

Cream together butter and sugar. Beat in eggs and vanilla and whip on high with mixer, for 5 minutes.

Mix together flour and other dry ingredients. Blend in at low speed, dry ingredients, one third at a time, alternately with cocoa mixture, starting and ending with flour. Beat only till mixed.

Bake in three 8"or 9" cake pans, greased and floured, at 350° for 25-30 minutes, till center is done. Cool in pans 10 minutes. Loosen with spatula and turn out on cooling rack to cool completely.

Intense Chocolate Frosting:
½ c. soft butter
8 oz. soft cream cheese
8 1 oz. squares, unsweetened baking chocolate, melted over hot water, cooled a bit
4 tsp. vanilla
6-8 Tbs. strong coffee
5 c. powdered sugar

Cream butter and cream cheese together well. Add rest at low speed, gathering momentum after sugar is blended, whip till smooth. Will be soft while spreading till set.

To assemble, place first layer, top side down, on cake plate. Slather on a thick layer of chocolate frosting. Add another layer of cake. Ditto on the frosting. Place last layer on top, top side up. Spread frosting on top and then down the sides, smoothing and swirling evenly.

Of course, a cake spatula is the best tool, with the bend in it. But any long, thin metal spatula is better than a rubber spatula for this noble task. You could decorate with nuts or such, but it's not needed for this momentous statement of supreme chocolate, with tender, rich cake.

Apricot-Coconut Cake

8 oz. soft cream cheese
½ c. soft butter
1¼ c. sugar
¼ c. milk
2 eggs
1 tsp. vanilla
1¾ c. flour
1 tsp. baking powder
½ tsp. baking soda
¼ tsp. salt
1 18 oz. jar apricot jam

Cream cream cheese, butter and sugar together well. Beat in milk, vanilla and eggs. Mix dry ingredients together and add to creamed mix.

Spread one half of batter in greased and floured 9"x 12" baking pan. Dot with jam and cover with rest of batter.

Bake at 350° for 35-40 minutes, until center is set.

Topping: Combine:
  2 c. coconut
  ½ c. packed brown sugar
  1/3 c. butter, melted
  1 tsp. cinnamon

Spread on cake and broil until golden brown.

Easy Apple Cake mit Streusel

Beat together till smooth:
  2 c. sugar
  1 c. oil
  2 tsp. vanilla
  2 eggs
  1 tsp. baking soda
  1 tsp. cinnamon

Beat in:
  2½ c. flour
  3 c. chopped tart apples' peeled

Spread in greased, floured 9"x 12" pan. Sprinkle streusel on top, bake 350°, 50-60 minutes.

Streusel Topping:
  ½ c. brown sugar
  ½ c. flour
  1-2 tsp. cinnamon
  4 Tbs. soft butter
Cream together with fingers.

Good warm with whipped cream.

Pear Cake

½ c. soft butter
1½ c. sugar
4 egg yolks
½ c. mashed canned pears
1 tsp. vanilla
1 c. sour cream
2 c. flour
1 tsp. baking soda
4 egg whites, beaten stiff but not dry
☺ canned or fresh pear slices
2 c. whipping cream, whipped stiff with 4 Tbs. sugar

Cream butter and sugar till light. Beat in yolks, mashed pears and vanilla. Blend in flour and baking soda. Fold in egg whites. Bake in greased and floured tube pan at 350° for 40-50 minutes.

When cool, frost with whipped cream and arrange pear slices, overlapping around top. Sprinkle with toasted, chopped nuts and/or drizzle with caramel or chocolate sauce.

Date Sugar Apple Cake

No white sugar, but oh so sweet!

½ c. cold butter
2 c. flour
1 Tbs. baking powder
½ tsp. salt
1 c. date sugar
¾ c. milk
1 egg
4 c. apples, chopped small
½ c. maple syrup
½ c. apple juice concentrate
1 tsp. cinnamon

Mix together flour, baking powder, salt and date sugar. Cut in butter to the texture of coarse corn meal. Whip together milk and egg and fold into the dry mix. On lightly floured board, gently shape dough to fit a non-metal 9"x 9" baking dish.

Melt butter in the baking dish in the oven. Mix syrup and apple juice together and mix into the butter. Spread apples in pan evenly. Cover and bake in oven at 350° for 20 minutes.

Remove from oven and place the cake dough over the apples. Bake at 425° for 20 minutes. Invert immediately onto serving platter and remove pan.

Good hot or cold, with or without honey sweetened whipped cream.

Date Sugar Pear Cake

No white sugar, and delicious!

½ c. soft butter
1¼ c. date sugar + ¼ c. for top
1½ c. flour
½ tsp. baking powder
1 tsp. baking soda
½ c. buttermilk
¾ c. apple juice concentrate
2 c. cut up ripe pears (2)
½ tsp. nutmeg

Cream butter and 1 c. date sugar till fluffy. Beat in next 5 ingredients. Fold in pears. Spread in 9"x 9" greased baking pan. Sprinkle with ¼ c. date sugar and nutmeg.

Bake at 350° about 30 minutes, till firm in middle. Serve hot or cold, with cream.

Fruit and Nut Loaf
2 large loaves

1½ c. soft butter
2½ c. sugar
4 eggs
3 c. flour
½ tsp. baking powder
1 tsp. salt
¾ c. milk
1 Tbs. vanilla
1 c. golden raisins
1 c. coarse chopped pecans
½ c. currants
½ c. whole, blanched almonds
½ - ¾ lb. dried apricots or pears
½ - ¾ lb. dried peaches
20 candied cherries
20 whole, pitted dates

Cream butter and sugar light and fluffy. Beat in eggs. Beat in flour, baking powder, salt, milk and vanilla. Mix in currants, raisins and nuts.

Grease 2 large loaf pans. Line with wax paper and grease again,. Spread one third of batter between bottoms of both pans. Arrange dried apricots, packed close together, end-on-end, along the sides. Fill in the middles with dates, close as possible.

Spread another third carefully over tops of fruit. Arrange dried peaches same way along the sides, with cherries end-on-end down the middle. Spread with last third of batter.

Bake at 325° for about an hour, till toothpick stuck in middle comes out clean. Cool and pull off paper.

Ice with Powdered Sugar Icing Glaze and decorate with candied cherries.

Apple Juice Gingerbread

Wonderful with whipped cream and no white sugar!

2½ c. flour
1 tsp. baking soda
1½ tsp. ginger
1 tsp. cinnamon
½ tsp. salt
¾ c. apple juice concentrate
½ c. butter
1 c. molasses
1 egg

Mix dry ingredients together in a bowl. Heat apple juice and stir in butter till melted. Mix into dry ingredients with molasses and egg.

Bake in greased 9"x 9" pan at 350° about 40-50 minutes, or till done in middle. Serve warm with whipped cream sweetened with maple syrup

Old-Tyme Gingerbread

2 c. flour
1½ tsp. ginger
1¼ tsp. cinnamon
½ tsp. each: cloves, nutmeg and salt
2 tsp. baking powder
2 eggs, well beaten
¾ c. packed brown sugar
¾ c. molasses
¾ c. butter
1 c. boiling water
½ tsp. baking soda

Mix first 7 ingredients together in separate bowl. Pour boiling water over butter and molasses in bowl and mix well to melt butter. Stir in baking soda.

Mix in dry ingredients and beat till smooth. Bake in greased 9"x 9" baking pan, at 350°, for 40 minutes, until done in middle. Serve warm or cold, with whipped cream and/or Rhubarb Sauce.

Rhubarb Sauce:
1 lb. chopped fresh or frozen rhubarb
1 c. water
1 c. sugar

Heat water and stir in sugar to melt. Add rhubarb and cook, stirring occasionally, medium heat, till rhubarb is tender and falling apart.

A very delicious, easy, tangy sauce.

All the following frosting recipes frost and decorate
one 9" 2-layer cake

Basic Buttercream Frosting

1 c. butter or margarine, soft
1 lb. powdered sugar
2 tsp. vanilla, or other extract
3-4 Tbs. milk

Basic method is to put it all in a bowl and let the fur fly! You do have to start on low speed (so it doesn't fly too much), and turn the mixer up gradually. Start with 3 Tbs. milk and add more if needed.

Eventually, as you cream and cream, you can watch the magical change as a rather coarse texture becomes smooth, creamy and refined.

If you want to be more sedate about it, cream the butter or margarine, gradually beating in the powdered sugar, and then the milk and flavorings.

Chocolate Frosting

Add to Basic Buttercream:
 2/3-¾ c. unsweetened baking
   cocoa
To make it extra rich and glossy, add 1 egg while beating.

Lemon or Orange Frosting

Use Basic Buttercream and add grated peel from 1 or 2 lemons or oranges. Use lemon or orange extract rather than vanilla, and lemon or orange juice instead of milk. Undiluted concentrate is good.

Cream Cheese Frosting

8 oz. softened cream cheese
½ c. soft butter
1-2 tsp. vanilla
1 lb. powdered sugar

Cream cream cheese and butter. Gradually add sugar and vanilla, and beat till light and creamy.

Cream Cheese Honey Frosting

Cream all together:
8 oz. softened cream cheese
½ c. soft butter
1/3 c. honey
1 tsp. vanilla
3 c. powdered sugar

Mocha Frosting

¾ c. soft butter or margarine
4 c. powdered sugar
3 Tbs. unsweetened baking
   cocoa
1 tsp. cinnamon, if desired
1 tsp. vanilla
1 egg yolk, if desired
4 tsp. instant coffee
   dissolved in:
3-4 Tbs. hot water

Cream together butter, sugar, cocoa, cinnamon and vanilla, adding coffee mix gradually as it creams, and egg towards the end.

White Chocolate Buttercream Frosting
Frosts a 9" cake

½   c. milk
1   c. sugar
3   Tbs. cornstarch
8   oz. white chocolate, chopped
1½ c. cold butter

Make a smooth paste with sugar, cornstarch and a little of the milk in a saucepan. Stir in rest of water. Cook, medium heat, stirring constantly, till thickened. Stir in white chocolate till melted. Cool to room temperature- can't be warm.

Cut butter into pieces, and, using mixer, whip butter into chocolate a piece at a time, till smooth and creamy.

Chocolate Glaze
A fudge-like covering when it cools. See page 159 for the recipe.

French Buttersilk Frosting I
Frosts 1 9" cake

Beat together:
1   c. soft butter
3   c. powdered sugar
1   Tbs. vanilla
Beat in 2 eggs, one at a time.

This silky smooth, rich frosting needs to be spread on the cake right away, before it develops air bubbles.

French Buttersilk Frosting II
For 9" cake

2/3 c. sugar
¼   c. flour
♥   pinch salt
¾   c. milk
1   tsp. vanilla
1   c. unsalted butter, chilled

Mix sugar, flour, salt in saucepan and mix in milk till smooth. Cook over medium heat with constant stirring until very thick. Turn into a mixing bowl and cool to room temperature.

Don't melt the butter! Taking one stick at a time out of fridge, cut into 4 pieces. Beat in 1 piece at a time, beating smooth after each addition. Beat in vanilla when all is smooth. Chill 5-10 minutes before spreading.

To make a coffee flavor, add 1 Tbs. instant coffee granules to milk in saucepan.

Whipped Cream Frosting

3   c. whipping cream, whipped, frosts 1 9" cake
4   c. whipping cream, whipped, frosts and lavishly decorates a 9" cake.

Sweeten each cup of cream with 2 Tbs. sugar, added before whipping, and a dash of vanilla, if desired. Chill beaters and bowls. Beat till stiff, but don't overbeat- you'll have butter.

Creamy Caramel Icing
9" layer cake

Heat together to melt butter:
- 1/3 c. whipping cream
- 6 Tbs. butter

Caramelize:
- 2 Tbs. sugar by melting in heavy pan over low heat, stirring constantly till golden brown.

Add hot milk and butter to sugar and mix till smooth.

Beat in:
- 3 c. powdered sugar
- 1 tsp. vanilla

to a smooth and creamy consistency, easy to spread.

Brown Sugar Frosting
9" layer cake

- 2¾ c. brown sugar
- 2/3 c. whipped cream
- 2/3 c. butter
- 1½ c. powdered sugar
- 1 tsp. vanilla

Melt and stir together in large saucepan, first 3 ingredients. Bring to a rolling boil. Cook, medium heat, stirring, for 2-3 minutes.

Cool to warm and beat in sugar and vanilla till creamy and smooth. Spread while still warm.

Chocolate Mousse Whipped Cream
9" layer cake

- 4 c. whipping cream, chilled
- ¾ c. unsweetened baking cocoa- or more depending on how intense you want it.
- 2/3 to ¾ c. sugar
- 1 tsp. vanilla

Add cocoa, sugar and vanilla to cream and whip. Halfway thru, when the cocoa is more or less incorporated, taste, to decide whether to add more or adjust the cocoa/sugar ratio. Finish whipping to soft, spreadable texture. Chocolate whips up faster than plain whipped cream, so don't wait too long to adjust the flavor. Keep chilled. Best served the same day, but still good next day.

Raspberry Creme
9" layer cake

- 3 c. whipping cream, chilled
- 2 c. fresh or frozen (thawed) raspberries, unsweetened
- ¼ c. raspberry jam

Sweeten to taste, starting with 1/3 c. sugar. Whip all together to soft peaks, adjusting sugar.

Slather between layers and all over outside.

Intense Cream Cheese Chocolate Frosting

See the recipe: Three Layer Chocolate Cake with Cream Cheese Chocolate Frosting. You won't be disappointed.

All following fillings will fill a 9" 2-layer cake

Custard Filling

1½ c. milk
½ c. sugar
4½ Tbs. flour
4 egg yolks, or 2 whole eggs, beaten
2 tsp. vanilla
1 Tbs. butter

Mix sugar and flour together in saucepan and make a paste with a little of the milk. When smooth, add rest of milk. Heat to boiling over medium heat, stirring constantly. Remove from heat when thick & bubbly.

Pour thin stream of hot milk into beaten eggs, whisking constantly. When a third of the sauce is incorporated, return all to pan, and, mixing well, bring back to boiling point. Cook one minute. Remove from stove and stir in vanilla and butter. Cool with buttered (on inside) plastic wrap covering top. Chill.

For deluxe filling: When chilled, fold in ½ c. whipping cream, whipped to sturdy peaks.

Maple Mousse Filling

no white sugar!
Cream all together:
3 oz. soft cream cheese
1/3 c. maple syrup
1 tsp. maple extract

Fold in: ¾ c. whipping cream, whipped with 4 Tbs. maple syrup, to soft peaks.

Ricotta Filling

2 c. ricotta cheese
2/3 c. powdered sugar
1 tsp. vanilla
1/3 c. chopped maraschino cherries
1/3 c. chopped, dried apricots
2 oz. semi-sweet chocolate, chopped small
1 Tbs. minced, candied ginger, if desired

Beat ricotta, powdered sugar and vanilla till creamy. Fold in rest and chill.

Fruit and Nut Filling

Using:
1 c. of Basic Buttercream Frosting
Fold in 4 choices of following:
¼ c. crushed macaroons
¼ c. coconut (try toasted)
¼ c. chopped pecan (ditto)
¼ c. chopped almonds (ditto)
¼ c. chopped maraschino cherries
¼ c. chopped other dried fruit, such as pineapple or apricot

Powdered Sugar Icing Glaze

To:
1 c. powdered sugar
Beat in:
2-3 Tbs. milk, or lemon juice, or orange juice

Add last half of liquid drop by drop to bring it to a smooth-flowing but not too thin consistency. Doesn't take much to make it runny, but if it does just add a little powdered sugar.

Further Confessions

It is so embarrassing, but I must confess we made the cherry pies with canned cherry pie filling. Lots of butter and a top crust of overlapping pie crust scraps (there were lots of those), sprinkled with cinnamon and sugar, were the tour de force that disguised this awful truth. But they tasted so good! Forgiven?

And tho I use butter in everything else, I did use margarine in the pie crust and buttercream frosting.- Buttery but not butter! So sorry!

I still find it shudderingly amazing that during those great big trade fairs we made close to 40-50 pies a day, served up at lunch- That is 400 pieces eaten in 3 hours! And they all came from a small, 8'x14', kitchen with an old, oversized stove I picked up in some yard sale. When the oven door was open, you couldn't pass. It blocked the way. My kids tortured me by wanting to trot on by when the oven was open. They say I tortured them!

We had it down to a science. I made piles of pie crusts (10 recipes at a time in a big mixing bowl) rolled them out and froze them sandwiched between wax paper. We peeled and cut bags and bags of fresh Granny Smith apples (using the handy apple corer-peeler-slicer) and froze those too. The kids were good at that task and even sort of liked it. There were apple peel fights. Then came the assembly line: My husband mixed big bowls of fruit filling(or opened cans of cherries) and shoved it my way. I filled, covered and crimped (there is an art to crimping) and threw them back his way. He fields and fills the oven. We packed 6 in at a time, staggered, and half way thru the baking process, switched them around so they cooked evenly. We both watched the baking progress so as not to space and burn all the good work.

Daughter was the official cream whipper, which she wasn't too thrilled about. She still is, but she says it's not so bad now. That's progress!

Pie Crust
For a 2-crust 9"or10" pie
I often get asked how to make a successful pie crust. It seems a worthwhile
endeavor to explain "the secret," step by step.

¾ c. butter or good quality margarine, chilled
2 c. flour
½ tsp. salt
up to 4 Tbs. ice water (measure out ¼ c. and drop in ice cube)

Mix flour and salt in medium sized bowl and cut in butter with a pastry cutter. (The best pastry cutters have semi-circled rows of wire attached to both ends of a handle. I like the shape of the older ones and find those in antique stores and specialty shops.) Cut straight in-don't smear-and toss loose flour up from bottom until it resembles a coarse meal with pea size particles.

Sprinkle water over the mix, using a tablespoon at a time. I use a large wooden paddle to mix in the water, tossing and pressing the dough together rather than stirring like a cake batter. (The tossing brings out the loose flour to mix with the water.) It should be pressed together, not smeared. It takes a little time for the water to distribute and particles to adhere, but if you need to you can add 1-2 more Tbs. water. Don't go over the allotted water too much or dough will be rubbery.

And don't use your hands to mix, as the warmth will melt the layering of fat and flour. The layering creates the flakiness.

As the dough finally comes together, form it into 2 semi-flattened balls, ready to roll. Chill an hour, covered. Sprinkle rolling area lightly with flour. Roll out one patty of dough, starting from the center and rolling out in all directions, adding a little more pressure to the thicker areas. Flour lightly wherever it might stick, including roller. If is splits around the edges, you can roll one side of a split edge, twisting the rolling pin towards the other edge, pinching the two sides back together.

When the dough is almost half rolled out, gently lift it and sprinkle more flour underneath. Finish rolling a circle somewhat larger than your pie plate. Fold in half and carefully lift into your pie plate, unfolding.

If making a single pie crust, trim the edge to overlap an inch. Fold under the edge so the dough sits on top of the lip flush with the edge of pie plate. Shape so it's even and crimp as below.

If making a 2-crust pie, trim the bottom dough so it sags evenly over the edge just a bit. Roll out second patty in same manner. Fill with filling and arrange crust over the top. Evenly trim to overlap 1". Tuck top overlapped edge under the bottom crust edge and pinch into an even shape, sealing as you go. Then crimp.

Crimp edges by holding thumb and forefinger against outside edge. Use forefinger of other hand, positioned on other side of same edge, pressing pie dough between pinched fingers of first hand, forming a vee in the crust. Repeat all around to make a fluted edge.

Make several slashes in top crust before baking, for steam escapeage.

For your now crimped single pie crust, (to be filled after baking), pierce shell all over with many fork holes. Place sheet of foil in shell and fill with dry beans. Bake at 375°, 10-15 minutes. Carefully lift foil and beans out. Continue baking another 10 minutes, till golden. Beans keep crust from shrinking, as do fork holes.

Pie dough will stay up to a week in fridge and a couple months in freezer.

Sound tricky? Just try it a few times and it will roll into place!

Fresh Apples Pie
10" pie plate

1 pie crust recipe

Mix all together:
- 9 c. peeled, cored, sliced tart baking apples (Rome, Macintosh, Granny Smith, Golden Delicious)
- 1 c. sugar
- 1/3 c. flour
- 1 tsp. cinnamon

Pour into pie crust and dot with:
- 3 Tbs. cold butter

Cover with second crust. Seal, crimp and slash.

You could sprinkle with cinnamon and sugar, or not.

Bake at 350° for 45 minutes, or so, till brown and bubbly and apples are tender when pierced with a fork.

Let set 20 minutes, if you can, before cutting.

Apple Juice Sweetened Apple Pie
10" pie plate

No white sugar and just as good!

1 pie crust recipe
9 c. apples, as in last recipe
1 12 oz. can apple juice
concentrate
2/3 c. flour

1 tsp. cinnamon
2-3 Tbs. butter

Other than those couple of changes, this one's the same as Fresh Apples Pie recipe.

Blackberry Pie
9" deep dish

1 pie crust recipe
2 1 lb. bags frozen blackberries
11/3 c. sugar
½ c. flour
3 Tbs. butter

Partially defrost berries before mixing with sugar and flour (otherwise sugar and flour don't stick and end up a mass at bottom of pie). Follow Apple Pie recipe. Bake 35-40 minutes.

Blackberry-Peach Pie
9" deep dish

1 pie crust recipe
1 29 oz. can sliced peaches, drained and squished (like mud thru the fingers)
1 1 lb. bag blackberries, partially thawed

¾ c. sugar
1/3 c. flour
1 tsp. cinnamon
2-3 Tbs. butter

Follow Apple Pie recipe. Bake 35-45 minutes.

Blackberry-Peach Pie, Fruit Juice Sweetened
9" deep dish
A little tart but just as good

1 recipe pie crust
Mix together:
1 29 oz. can unsweetened peaches, drained and squished
1 lb. bag frozen blackberries, thawed enuf to mix

2/3 c. flour
1 tsp. cinnamon

Use Apple Pie recipe. Bake 35-45 minutes.

Cherry-Peach Pie, Fruit Juice Sweetened
9" deep dish

1 pie crust recipe
1 32 oz. can unsweetened peaches, drained and smushed
1 1 lb. bag frozen, unsweetened pie cherries

1 12 oz. can apple juice concentrate, defrosted
½ c. flour
1 tsp. cinnamon
½ tsp. nutmeg
3 Tbs. cold butter

Mix as in Apple Pie recipe

Tutti-Frutti Pie
10" pie

1 recipe pie crust
1 29 oz. can peaches, drained and squished
1 16 oz. can tart pie cherries, drained, or 1 lb. bag frozen
1 c. blackberries

1 c. sliced apples
½ c. flour
1 c. sugar
1 tsp. cinnamon
3 Tbs. cold butter

Follow Apple Pie recipe.

Strawberry-Rhubarb Pie
10" pie

1 recipe pie crust
4 c. fresh or frozen rhubarb, chopped, thawed
4 c. strawberries, fresh or frozen, partially thawed
2 c. sugar

2/3 c. flour
½ tsp. nutmeg
½ tsp. cinnamon
3 Tbs. butter

Same procedure as Apple Pie

Rhubarb Custard Pie
10" pie

1 recipe pie crust
2 1 lb. bags frozen rhubarb, thawed, or 8 c. fresh, chopped
2 eggs beaten
2 c. sugar

½ c. whipping cream
½ c. flour
1 tsp. nutmeg
2 Tbs. cold butter

The usual, but beat the eggs and cream together first. Mix all.

Apple-Cranberry Pie
9" pie

1 recipe pie crust

Mix in a large bowl:
6 c. tart, baking apples
    peeled and sliced
¾ c. sugar
½ c. flour

At end fold in:
1 16 oz. can whole cranberry
    sauce

Dot with 2-3 Tbs. cold butter
Proceed as in Apple Pie recipe,
except bake maybe 10 minutes
less.

Peach Streusel Pie
9" pie

½ recipe pie crust, arranged
    and crimped in pie plate

Mix and fill pie shell with:
2 29 oz. cans peaches,
    drained and sliced
    or 6-7 c. fresh, sliced
½ c. sugar
½ c. flour
½ tsp. cinnamon

Streusel: Mix together:
½ c. soft butter
2/3 c. flour
1 c. packed brown sugar
1 tsp. cinnamon
½ tsp. nutmeg

Distribute streusel evenly over
peaches. Bake at 350°, about 40
minutes, until bubbly and crispy on
top.

Pumpkin Pie
9" pie

Mix all together:
1 16 oz. can canned pumpkin
¾ c. sugar
3 eggs
11/3 c. half & half or evaporated
    milk
2 tsp. cinnamon
1½ tsp. ground ginger
1 tsp. nutmeg
½ tsp. cloves

Mix together well and pour into
prepared unbaked pie shell.

Bake at 350° for 45-50 minutes,
till knife inserted in center comes
out clean.

This is my son's favorite. He makes it
himself now, tho his pie crust does
need a little help. He is getting to be
a good cook!

Pecan Pie
9" pie

1 unbaked pie shell, crimped and all

Cream together till smooth:
11/3 c. light corn syrup
1 c. packed brown sugar
1 tsp. vanilla

¼ c. butter, melted
5 eggs
Add:
11/3 c. pecan halves

Pour in filling and bake at 350° for 45 minutes, till set.

Buttermilk Custard Pie
10" pie

1 baked 10" pie shell, following directions in Pie Crust recipe

Whisk together well, till smooth:
½ c. flour
2 Tbs. butter, melted
6 egg yolks
1½ c. sugar
3 c. buttermilk
1 c. half & half
2 tsp. lemon extract

After beating till smooth, taste to see if you want more sugar.

Pour into cooled shell and bake at 425° for 10 minutes. Reduce heat to 350° and bake another 45-50 minutes, till knife inserted in middle comes out clean.

This is an awesome tasting pie. Don't be put off by the buttermilk.

Frozen Raspberry Pie
9" pie

Crust: Cream together:
½ c. soft butter
¼ c. brown sugar
1 c. flour

Spread mix in 8" square pan and bake at 400° for 15 minutes. Cool, crumble and press into 9" pie pan.

Filling:
1 c. sugar
3 unbeaten egg whites

10-12 oz. frozen raspberries', thawed and drained well
1 c. whipping cream, whipped stiff

Using mixer, whip berries, sugar and egg whites at high speed for 15 minutes. Fold in cream. Pile in pie shell and freeze overnight.

A divinely tasting confection, light and airy. And it does whip up.

No-Bake Cheesecake Pie
9" pie

1   single pie crust in 9" pie plate, baked according to directions in Pie Crust recipe, baked crispy and light brown

Filling:
Cream till fluffy:
- 8   oz. soft cream cheese
- 1   can sweetened condensed milk

Add and mix well:
- 1/3   c. fresh lemon or lime juice

Pour into cooled pie shell and refrigerate several hours.

Fruit topping:
1   to 1½ lbs. of your favorite fresh or frozen fruit, such as strawberries, blackberries, raspberries, peaches, cherries, kiwi or blueberries.
- ½   pt. whipping cream, whipped firm with 2 Tbs. sugar

Spread fruit amply on top of chilled filling. If using a tart fruit, such as berries, sprinkle with a little sugar. If using frozen, allow at least an hour of refrigerator time before serving, so fruit can thaw some and not be icy- but not too soggy either.

Custard Pie
9" pie

- ½   recipe pie crust
- 1   Tbs. soft butter
- 4   eggs
- ½   c. sugar
- ½   tsp. salt
- 2½   c. scalded milk
- 1   tsp. vanilla
- ⅗   nutmeg

Prepare an unbaked 9" pie shell. Chill well. Rub soft butter on shell to keep custard from baking soggy.

Mix together eggs, salt and sugar. Slowly stir in hot milk; add vanilla and mix well. Pour into shell and sprinkle with nutmeg. Bake on lower shelf of oven at 425°, for 25 minutes, or until knife comes out clean from center.

Coconut variation:
Sprinkle ½ cup coconut on bottom of shell before adding custard mix.

Just Desserts and Last Confessions

I'll tell you my worst experience. A certain entrepreneur in town was having a birthday. This was to be an all out affair with several hundred people, and I was to do the cake. The desire was for an incredible tiered strawberry and whipped cream cake big enough to feed everyone.

I worked long and diligently all day on a beautiful cream-frosted 3-tiered cake (and many side cakes), covered thickly with the most gorgeous ever large and tasty strawberries. Upside-down long stem glasses separated the tires with elegant finesse.

As I am feverishly putting on the last touches on this extravaganza, my buddy, Carol, pops in the door and promptly sits in the seat that I had temporarily vacated. Carol is intent on her latest scheme and I am out of my position of watchfulness.

Suddenly, before our very eyes, the top two tiers sag to one side and topple onto the table in a crash of broken glass and smashed cake.- Utter silence. I truly wished I were dead or gone to Mexico (not my favorite place).

After a frozen 10 minutes I am back in the land of the living enough to assess the damage. Carol, being the good buddy, stayed to help. We bake cakes. We whip cream. We salvage and reposition.

I don't know why those cakes fell. I must have forgotten to put in a doweling. I never forget, except then? The other theory is the cake was too heavy and the doweling twisted. The only way we could get those cakes to work was to put the 12" almost on top of the 16", and no
glassware in between. First and last time it happened.
It was a good save. The expectations had to be changed a bit, but the strawberries were large and lucious, the cake delicious.
I even recovered enough to partake in the festivities. I won't tell you what happened to the company 3 months later.

Baklava

1 lb. fillo (22-24 sheets), thawed according to package directions
3-4 sticks butter, melted and hot

Filling: Mix all together:
3 c. walnuts, coarsely ground
2 c. almonds or hazelnuts, coarsely ground
¼ c. sugar
1 tsp. cinnamon
½ tsp. nutmeg
½ tsp. cloves
2 Tbs. melted butter

Have everything ready, including the filling, before unwrapping the fillo, as it dries out very quickly. Once unwrapped, keep it covered with wax paper when not using.

Use a 9"x 12" or 10"x 14" baking sheet or cake pan. Brush a sheet of fillo with butter. Fold in half, widthwise, and brush the top. Place in pan. Repeat with 4 more. Butter 4 more sheets but drape them half way over the 4 sides of pan.

Spread one third of filling over fillo in pan. Fold the draped sheets over the nuts.

Repeat with 2 folded sheets and 4 draped sheets of fillo. Spread with another third of nuts, and fold fillo over. Repeat once more. Finish off with rest of sheets, generously buttering top.

With sharp knife, score the top making 6 lengthwise strips. Then cut 10 strips diagonally widthwise, to form diamond shaped pieces. Pour any remaining butter over pastry.

Bake at 325° for 50-60 minutes. Cool 5 minutes and spoon half of cooled syrup (Siropi) over pastry.

Let sit 3 or more hours. Cut thru and thru where scored. Serve with rest of syrup.

Siropi
2 c. water
1½ c. sugar
½ of a lemon
½ of an orange
½ c. honey

Combine all in saucepan, except honey. Bring to a slow boil and cook over medium heat for 10 minutes. Stir in honey. Cool.

Apple Strudel
Makes 1 large strudel

Yeast dough:
- 1 pkg. dry active yeast
- ¼ c. warm water
- 1 tsp. sugar
- ¼ c. milk
- ¼ c. butter
- 1 Tbs. sugar
- ¾ tsp. salt
- 2½ c. flour
- 1 egg plus 1 egg yolk

Dissolve yeast in warm-hot water with 1 tsp. sugar for 10 minutes. Heat milk and butter. Mix in 1 Tbs. sugar and salt and cool to lukewarm. Mix 1 c. flour, yeast and eggs into milk mixture and beat smooth. Gradually add rest of flour, saving ½ c. for kneading. Turn out on well floured board and knead for 10-15 minutes, working in enough flour to make a smooth, satiny dough. Form into ball, oil, cover and chill for several hours.

Filling: Mix very well:
- 8 c. baking apples, finely chopped

- ¾ c. crushed walnuts
- ¾ c. golden raisins
- ¼ c. currants
- ¼ c. bread or cracker crumbs
- 1 c. sugar
- 1 Tbs. cinnamon
- ♥ grated peel of 1 lemon

To make strudel, let dough rest on board for 10 minutes. Roll to 15"x 20". Brush generously with:
- 1/3 c. melted butter

Spread filling evenly, leaving ½" margin on all sides. Drizzle with more butter. Roll pastry up, making a 15" long log. Dip finger in water and run along edges. Pinch to seal. Place on greased cookie sheet, seam side down, and form into horseshoe. Brush butter on dough before putting in oven, and halfway thru baking. Bake at 350° for 50 minutes. When cool, ice with glaze.

Glaze: Mix together:
- 2 c. powdered sugar
- 3 Tbs. fresh lemon juice

Apple Crisp

- 8 c. peeled, cored, sliced tart apples (Rome or Macintosh)
- 1 c. butter
- ½ brown sugar, not packed
- ½ c. sugar
- 2 c. flour

Cut butter and sugars and flour together well. Cream with fingers till crumbly/clumpy.

Mix apples with:
- ¼ c. flour
- ¾ c. sugar
- 1 tsp. cinnamon

Spread apples evenly in 9"x 12", non-metal baking pan. Sprinkle crumbles on top. Bake at 375° for 40-50 minutes, till apples are tender and basting in juices.

Apple Danish
20 squares

Pie pastry:
- 3 c. flour
- 1 tsp. salt
- 1¼ c. cold butter
- ½ c. milk

Follow Pie Crust recipe procedure. Divide dough in half, one half slightly larger. Roll large half to 12"x 17" and pat into bottom and sides of 10"x 15"baking sheet (fold into fourths to transfer).

Crumble over bottom crust:
- 1 c. corn flakes (or similar)

Top with:
- 9 c. tart apple slices (8-10)

Sprinkle with a mix of:
- ¾ c. sugar
- 1 tsp. cinnamon
- ♥ grated peel of 1 lemon

Roll second crust to fit top. Seal edges and crimp. Brush top with egg white and pierce with fork all over. Bake at 375° for 30 minutes, till crust is brown and apples are tender . Drizzle with icing while still a little warm. Cool and cut in squares, 4x5.

Icing: Blend till smooth:
- 1 full c. powdered sugar
- 3-4 Tbs. milk

Apple Dumpling
4 servings

- ½ recipe Pie Crust, rolled to large round, like 16"
- 4 large, tart baking apples (like Golden Delicious) peeled and cored
- ♥ Streusel Mix from Streusel Coffee Cake
- 1 egg

Drape pie crust over 9" pie plate. Stuff apple centers with streusel mix and place apples in center of pie plate and crust. Sprinkle with more streusel. Pull crust up and over the apples, wrapping apples completely. Pinch edges

together. Brush with egg beaten with 1 tsp. water. Bake at 350°, 45-50 minutes, until apples are tender.

Serve warm with Cinnamon Sauce Or try ice cream or whipped cream.

Cinnamon Sauce: Combine in saucepan and boil 2 minutes:
- ½ c. sugar
- 1 c. water
- 2 Tbs. butter
- ½ tsp. cinnamon

Apple Custard Bars
12 bars

Base:
- 2 c. flour
- 2 Tbs. sugar
- ¾ c. cold butter

Cut in butter with pastry cutter till crumbly. Press into ungreased 9"x 12" baking pan. Bake at 350° for 15 minutes.

Apple Layer:
- 6 c. thin sliced baking apples
- 1 c. sugar
- 1 tsp. cinnamon

Mix together and arrange on top of cookie crust. Bake, covered with tin foil, at 350° for 50-60 minutes, till tender when pierced with fork.

Custard layer:
- 2 Tbs. sugar
- 2 Tbs. cornstarch
- 3 egg yolks

- 2 c. half & half
- 1 tsp. vanilla

Mix sugar and cornstarch in saucepan. Add a little half & half to make a smooth paste. Add rest of half & half and egg yolks. Cook over medium heat, stirring, till mixture comes to a boil and thickens. Stir in vanilla. Pour over baked apples.

Meringue Topping:
- 3 egg whites
- ½ tsp. cream of tartar
- ½ c. sugar

In clean, medium bowl (won't whip if bowl is greasy), whip egg whites until soft peaks form. Beat in 1 Tbs. sugar at a time until stiff, glossy peaks form. Spread over custard to edges of pan. Bake at 350° for 20-25 minutes until light golden brown. Cool and serve.

Lemon Pudding Cake

Mix together:
- ½ c. flour
- 1½ c. sugar
- ½ tsp. salt
- ☺ grated peel, 1 large lemon

Stir in:

- ½ c. fresh lemon juice
- 3 egg yolks
- 1½ c. milk

Fold in:
- 3 egg whites, beaten till stiff

Pour into 9"x 9", non-metal baking pan or 2 qt. baking dish. Set in larger pan filled with 1" of hot water. Bake at 350° for 35-45 minutes, till set and brown. Serve warm or cold, with or without whipped cream.

Luscious lemon and delicate cake!

Danish Pastry
2 logs, 8-10 servings

Crust:
- 1 c. flour
- ½ c. butter
- 2 Tbs. cold water

Cut flour and butter together till mixture resembles coarse meal. Press in water sprinkled on top till all holds together in a ball. Divide dough in half. On an ungreased cookie sheet press out the 2 pieces into 3"x 12" flat logs.

Spread:
- 2 Tbs. raspberry jam down center of each log, leaving 2" margin on both sides.

Puffy Top Crust: Place together in saucepan and boil till butter melts:
- 1 c. water
- ½ c. butter

Beat in quickly all at once till it leaves sides of pan:
- 1 c. flour

Beat in till glossy:
- 3 eggs

Divide in half and, using hands, shape dough, carefully spreading evenly over crust, sealing edges.

Bake at 350° for 45-55 minutes till puffy and brown. Cool and frost with icing, and sprinkle with toasted nuts.

Icing: Beat well together:
- 1 c. powdered sugar
- 1 Tbs. soft butter
- 1 tsp. vanilla
- 2-3 Tbs. cold milk or cream

Fudge Pudding Cake

Mix together in bowl:
- 2 c. flour
- 4 tsp. baking powder
- ½ tsp. salt
- 1½ c. sugar
- ½ c. unsweetened baking cocoa

Stir in:
- 1 c. milk
- 6 Tbs. butter, melted
- 1½ c. chopped nuts, if desired

Spread in 9"x 12" glass baking dish.

Sprinkle with a mix of:
- 2 c. brown sugar
- ½ c. unsweetened cocoa

Pour over entire batter:
- 3½ c. hot water (it really works)

Bake 45 minutes at 350°. Cake will be on top and sauce on bottom. Serve individual pieces, spooning sauce on top. Or invert whole cake onto deepish serving platter with sauce on top. Good with whipped cream.

Chocolate Filled Hazelnut Linzertorte

Crust:
- 2 c. powdered sugar
- 1 c. soft butter
- 1 egg
- 2¼ c. flour
- 1 tsp. baking powder
- 1¾ c. ground hazelnuts (7oz.)
- ¾ c. raspberry jam

Beat powdered sugar and butter till fluffy. Blend in egg, flour and baking powder. Stir nuts in by hand. Put aside 1 c. of dough. Press rest evenly over bottom and ¾" up sides of 10" spring-form pan. Spread jam over top of dough.

Filling:
- ½ c. chocolate chips, semi sweet

- 1 oz. unsweetened baking chocolate
- ½ c. soft butter
- ½ c. powdered sugar
- 2 eggs
- 1 tsp. vanilla

Melt chocolates over low heat, stirring till smooth. Set aside. Beat butter and powdered sugar till fluffy. Beat in eggs, one at a time. Blend in chocolate and vanilla. Pour over jam and spread evenly. Roll reserved crust into long, finger thick ropes and arrange them in a continuing spiral on top. Bake at 350° for 50 minutes, till crust is golden. Cool completely before removing from pan.

Chocolate Brownie Mocha Mousse

- ½ Chocolate Cookie recipe

Spread chocolate cookie dough in greased 10" springform pan. Bake at 350° for 30 minutes, until set. Cool and remove from pan. Chill.

Mocha Filling:
- 1½ c. semi-sweet chocolate chips
- 2 Tbs. unsweetened cocoa
- 2 tsp. instant coffee crystals
- ¼ c. cream
- 3 Tbs. butter
- 1 c. whipping cream

In small saucepan combine chips, cocoa, coffee, cream and butter. Mix and melt till smooth. Set aside to cool.

Whip the whipping cream stiff. While melted mix is still slightly warm and soft, gently fold it into cream. Pile onto crust and coax out to edges.

Garnish with more whipped cream and/or sliced, toasted almonds.

Chocolate Almond Torte

Intense and rich with melts-in-your-mouth texture

5	oz. semi-sweet baking chocolate
¼	c. water
2	tsp. instant coffee granules
5	eggs, separated
¼	tsp. cream of tartar
1½	c. sugar
2/3	c. soft butter
2	c. blanched, ground almonds (1/2 lb.)
½	c. matzo meal or fine cracker crumbs

Heat chocolate, water, coffee over low heat, blending till smooth. Set aside.

In large, clean, bowl, mix egg whites with cream of tartar and whip to stiff peaks. Set aside.

In bowl, beat sugar, butter and egg yolks about 1 minute. Beat in chocolate, crumbs and almonds. Fold in egg whites.

Bake in greased, cocoa dusted 10" springform pan at 325° for 90 minutes. Center should be firm when pressed gently. Cool. Serve dusted with powdered sugar.

Cream Puffs
12 large puffs

By special request from a certain David C.

Heat to boiling in saucepan:
  1   c. water
  ½   c. butter

Add, all in one lump, stirring vigorously:
  1   c. flour

Keep mixing till dough leaves sides of pan and forms a ball, about a minute. Cool.

Beat eggs in 1 at a time, till dough is smooth and velvety:
  4   eggs

Drop by spoon onto ungreased cookie sheet, 2"-3" apart. Bake at 400° for 45-50 minutes, until puffed, golden brown and dry. Cool, cut off top cap and pull out innards. (tasty) Fill with your favorite filling: whipped cream, chocolate whipped cream, custard, fruit and cream, or ice cream, or any combo of creative genius. (Custard filling's in the cake section) Replace top and sift powdered sugar over all, or drizzle with chocolate glaze.

Make large, small, round, long (eclairs). Make a ring or pile on top. Lots of fun.

Lemon Roll
8-10 slices

Easier than it might seem

Cake:
- 3 eggs
- 1 c. sugar
- ¼ c. cold water
- 1 tsp. vanilla
- 1 c. flour
- 2 tsp. baking powder
- ½ tsp. salt

In bowl, beat eggs at high speed until thick and lemon colored, about 5 minutes. Add sugar gradually, still beating. Stir in water and extract. Add flour, baking powder and salt and beat at low speed just till mixed.

Pour into well greased and floured 10"x 15" jelly roll pan or cookie sheet. Spread evenly. Bake at 375° for 10-12 minutes, till top springs back when lightly touched.

Run knife around edges and immediately turn out on large dish towel dusted with powdered sugar. Trim off any hard edges. Roll up cake in towel, to make a long, 15" log. Place on rack to cool completely.

Filling:
- ½ c. sugar
- 2 Tbs. cornstarch
- 2/3 c. water
- 1 egg yolk, slightly beaten
- ☺ grated peel of 1 lemon
- 4 Tbs. lemon juice
- 1 Tbs. butter

In saucepan, make a paste of sugar, cornstarch and a little of the water. When smooth, blend in rest of water and cook over medium heat, stirring constantly (here's where a sawed off spatula works good), until it comes to a boil. Blend about ½ c. sauce into egg. Return all to saucepan, stirring well, and reheat till bubbly. Stir in remaining ingredients and cool.

Carefully unroll cooled cake. The inside, tightest part might not completely unroll-leave it. Remove towel. Spread cake with filling, tucking some underneath the curl. Roll up again, loosely.

Chill, covered, in fridge, an hour. Spread with sweetened whipped cream, or lemon flavored Powdered Sugar Icing Glaze, or dust with powdered sugar just before serving.

More Desserts and Pastries

Sweetly Simple Fruit Tart

Sweet Crust:
- ½ c. soft butter
- ½ c. sugar
- 1¼ c. flour
- 1 tsp. vanilla
- 1 Tbs. cream

Cream butter and sugar together. Mix in flour with cream and vanilla till it holds together. Pat into bottom of a 10" springform pan. Bake at 375° for 15 minutes, till brown. Cool.

Filling:
- 3 oz. soft cream cheese
- ¼ c. sugar
- 2 Tbs. cream
- 1 tsp. vanilla

Whip cream cheese and sugar together, till fluffy. Beat in rest. Spread over crust. Chill.

Topping:
- 4 c. your favorite fresh or frozen fruit, such as kiwi, strawberry, peaches, cherries, or an assortment
- 8 oz. of jam or jelly of same color and persuasion
- 1-2 c. whipping cream, sweetened and whipped

Arrange fruit over cream cheese. Melt jam over low heat and spoon over fruit, covering all. Dollop whipped cream around edges. Chill before serving.

For frozen fruit, allow an hour defrost time on tart before serving, so not too chill, or mushy.

Blackberry Cobbler

Melt:
- ½ c. butter

Pour into 6 cup baking dish.

Beat together:
- 1 c. flour
- 1 c. sugar
- 1½ tsp. baking powder
- 1 c. milk

Pour over melted butter in dish. Don't stir.

Pour into center of batter:
- 2 c. blackberries

Sprinkle with:
- ½ c. sugar

Don't stir.

Bake at 375° for 45- 55 minutes, until done in middle. Half way thru, cut open center a bit to allow steam to escape.

Really good!

Chestnut Rum Soufflé
Serves 3-4

Served to me for the first time by a friend in our college days, Emily. Sitting out on the patio of her bungalow, surrounded by the grand grounds and estate of a huge, wandering villa up in the hills of Santa Barbara, overlooking the Pacific Ocean. What a setting. Wish I knew where Emily was now.

1 c. canned, sweet, chestnut puree
1-2 tsp. rum extract, or 2 Tbs. real rum
4 egg whites, at room temperature

If you could not find sweetened chestnut puree, sweeten it to taste with sugar or honey.

Beat the egg whites to stiff peaks. Mix in a swatch to the puree to lighten it up a bit and then carefully fold in the rest of the egg whites.

Pour into greased soufflé dish. Bake 45 minutes at 375°. Serve warm or cold with sweetened whipped cream. Yum.

Banana Fritters
4-6 servings

This is the kind of treat you want to transfer from skillet straight to waiting, held out plates. Luscious!

1 c. flour
1½ tsp. active dry yeast
☺ pinch salt
7/8 c. warm-hot water
2 Tbs. oil
1 egg white
4 large bananas
½ c. butter
☺ cinnamon, sugar

Combine flour, yeast and salt in bowl. Mix water and oil and gradually add to flour mix. Let rise at least 1 hour, covered, in warm place. Just before ready to make the fritters, beat egg white stiff and fold into batter.

Peel bananas and cut at a long slant about ½" thick, so you have thick slabs.

Melt butter 2 Tbs. at a time in large skillet, hot but not burning (Can add a little oil to help)

Dip bananas in batter- fingers work best-not letting it be too thick in coating. Fry in batches till brown, turning once. Add more butter as needed. Drain on paper towels and keep warm, if they last that long.

Sprinkle with cinnamon and sugar, if desired.

Try with apple slices, making the slices thinner, to cook faster.

Brownie Puddin' n' Pie

Melt:
½ c. butter
Beat in:
1 c. packed brown sugar
1 tsp. vanilla
1 egg
1 c. flour
1 tsp. baking powder
¼ tsp. salt
½ c. chopped nuts

Pour into greased 9"-10" pie plate and bake at 350°, 20-25 minutes, till golden brown. Cool.

Puddin' n' Pie Filling:
1 10 oz. bar, white chocolate, chopped
1/3 c. whipping cream
1 c. whipping cream, whipped with 1 tsp. vanilla extract
♥ Macadamia nuts- as many as you can afford!

Melt chocolate with 1/3 c. cream. Cool to room temperature and fold into whipped cream. Spread onto brownie crust and sprinkle toasted macadamias on top. Chill.

Fill with Puddin' n' Pie Filling, or your favorite pudding, or ice cream (freeze all), or chocolate whip cream, or any other surprises you can think of. Good

Richly Braised Pears
6-8 servings
Good recipe for all those local pears hanging on trees in the fall.

6-8 firm pears, peeled, halved, cored
1/3 c. sugar
3 Tbs. cold butter
2 c. whipping cream
2-3 Tbs. honey
½ tsp. vanilla

Place pears cut side down in 9"x 12" baking pan. Sprinkle with sugar and dot with butter. Bake 40 minutes at 400°, or until tender.

Reduce heat to 350°. Pour 1 cup of cream over pears and return to oven. Bake 10 minutes until sauce is thick and caramel colored, basting pears a few times while cooking. Cool a bit.

Whip rest of cream with honey and vanilla to soft peaks. Serve pears with dollops of cream.

Custard in Fillo
32 pieces
This is a very ethnic, eggy tasting pastry. I love its flavor and uniqueness.

1   lb. fillo, thawed
1   c. butter, melted and hot
2   c. Siropi (see index)

Filling:
½   c. butter
4½   c. milk
½   c. regular farina

Mix together and set aside:
6   large eggs
½   c. sugar
1   grated orange rind
1   tsp. vanilla

In a large saucepan, bring milk and butter to a boil. Stirring constantly, add farina and cook, stirring 5 minutes. Remove from heat and gradually add about 1 c of hot mix, whisking well. Return all to saucepan and cook a few minutes, till thick and smooth. Cool completely

Brush 9"x 12" baking pan with butter. Butter and layer 8 sheets fillo in pan, folding them in half, widthwise. Drape 4 buttered, folded in half sheets over all four sides. Spread filling in pan. Fold the overlapping sheets over filling. Cover with remaining, buttered, sheets. Butter top. Score lines 4x8 and pour on rest of butter.

Bake 350° for 50-60 minutes, till golden and puffed. Cool 5 minutes and spoon on ½ of syrup. Cut thru and serve with rest of syrup. Good warm or cold.

Fruit and Creme
4 servings

Fabulous, and with no white sugar!

Whip together:
8   oz. soft cream cheese
½   c. orange juice

Whip together in another bowl to soft and sturdy folds:
1   c. whipping cream
2   Tbs. honey or maple syrup

Fold cream and cheese together. Layer with 2-3 c. fruit in 4 dessert cups. Chill and serve.

Almond Rice Creme
5-6 servings

Wonderfully light and exotic! From Annie Woozle

¼ c. white long grain rice
2 c. milk

Cook over low heat, stirring often, covered first half, about 30 minutes total, until tender.

Add, blend in and chill:
½ c. sugar
3 Tbs. cream sherry
1 tsp. vanilla
½ tsp. almond extract

Fold in:
1 c. whipping cream, whipped to soft but sturdy folds

Place in serving bowl and sprinkle over top:
½ c. toasted, slivered almonds
(Bake almonds at 300° 7-10 minutes.) Chill an hour or so.

Tortoni
12 cupcake servings

A no white sugar delicious treat, that my daughter asks for every Christmas.

1 c. half & half
3 oz. soft cream cheese
½ c. honey, or 1/3 c. sugar, or 1/3 c. maple syrup plus 2 Tbs. apple juice concentrate
1 tsp. vanilla
½ tsp. almond extract
½ c. toasted, chopped almonds or pecans
¼ c. finely chopped dates
1 c. chopped fruit of choice, such as sweet cherries

Cream cream cheese and honey till smooth. Add rest. Pour into cup cake paper lined muffin tins. Freeze 4-5 hours, or till hard.

(Picture a kid sitting on a back porch steps, peeling back the paper one bite at a time.)

Maple Cream
6-8 servings

No white sugar, and absolutely divine!

1   c. whipping cream, whipped
    with 2 Tbs. maple syrup, to
    sturdy folds
6   oz. soft cream cheese,
    whipped with 2 Tbs. maple
    syrup
1   c. sour cream

Fold all together and chill several hours, covered.

Wonderful served with fresh fruit, such as peeled and sliced oranges, grapes, peaches, sweet cherries.

Try layering with fruit in dessert cups.

Classic Cheesecake via New York
12-16 servings

Crust:
2   c. rubbed cake crumbs

Thickly butter the bottom of a 10" springform pan. Press in cake crumbs.

Filling:
4   eggs
2   c. cottage cheese
24 oz cream cheese
1½ c. sugar
6   Tbs. flour
1   Tbs. fresh lemon juice
♥   grated peel of 1 lemon
2   tsp. vanilla
2   c. sour cream mixed with
    ¼ c. sugar

Blend eggs and cottage cheese in blender till smooth. Whip cream cheese and sugar together till light and fluffy. Mix all ingredients together till smooth, leaving out the sour cream

Fill pan with mixture and smooth top. Place in middle of oven. Place pan filled with hot water on lower oven rack. Bake at 325° for 60 or 70 minutes. Spread sweetened sour cream over top and return to oven for 10 minutes.

Turn off heat and leave in oven till cool, with door open, covered loosely with tin foil.

Chill well, at least 4-5 hours.

Fluffier cheesecake. Dense cheesecake is great but so is this: Just separate the eggs and cream the cottage cheese with egg yolks and vanilla. Mix in rest of stuff, except sour cream. Whip the egg whites to very frothy (very clean beaters) and gradually beat in ¼ c. sugar till stiff peaks form. Fold into rest of mixture. Bake. Do sour cream. Very light, creamy.

Light and Lively Lemon Cheesecake

Crust:
- 1 c. flour
- ¼ c. brown sugar, not packed
- ½ c. soft butter

Cream together with wooden spoon and press on bottom and 1" up sides of 10" springform pan. Bake at 400° for 12 minutes Cool.

Filling:
- 24 oz. soft cream cheese (3 8 oz. packages)
- 1¼ c. sugar
- 4 egg yolks
- 1/3 c. flour
- 2/3 c. fresh lemon juice (3-5 lemons)
- 1 Tbs. grated lemon peel

- 4 egg whites
- ¼ c. sugar

In large mixing bowl, cream the cream cheese smooth. Gradually add sugar, then beat on high for 3 minutes, till light and fluffy. Beat in egg yolks, flour, lemon juice and zest.

In separate bowl, (with very clean beaters,) whip the egg whites to soft peaks. Gradually add ¼ c. sugar and beat till stiff peaks form. Fold the egg whites into the cheese mix.

Wrap bottom and up the sides of springform in tin foil. Place pan in a larger pan. Fill springform pan with batter, smoothing top. Fill outside pan with 1" hot water. (Springform is now sitting in a hot water bath with tin foil to protect it from soaking up water.) Place in center of hot oven and bake at 350° for 80 minutes. Let cool on rack for several hours. Spread with glaze, then refrigerate overnight.

Lemon Glaze:
- 1 c. sugar
- ¼ c. cornstarch
- ½ tsp. salt
- 1 c. water
- 2 Tbs. grated lemon peel
- ½ c. lemon juice
- 3 Tbs. butter

Combine all but butter in medium saucepan and whisk over medium heat about 1 to 3 minutes, till thickish and smooth. The sauce will turn clear. Remove from heat and beat in butter with that wooden spoon. Cover and cool to warm before spreading.

Loosen sides of springform with sharp knife before removing from pan. Cut with a serrated knife dipped in hot water before each cut. Makes life easier.

If you want a less intense lemon flavor, use half lemon juice and half water or milk. But us lemon lovers will want it just the way it is!

Trade Fair Trifle
10-12 servings

This is a good chance to use up those extra unfrosted cakes lying around. At least I had them lying around. And, it is a delicious celebratory chance to use up all those other tasty odds and ends. So feel free to use your poetic license.

1   single layer of cake, split in half, lengthwise
♥   raspberry jam, or apricot
1   16 oz. can sliced peaches, chopped small (or fresh)
1   16 oz. can crushed pineapple
1   16 oz. can lemon pie filling or 1 recipe Custard Filling
2   c. fresh or frozen raspberries
2   c. whipping cream, whipped firm with ¼ c. sugar

Place one cake half in nice serving bowl. Now is the time to spread jam, if you want it. Next, spread half the custard or lemon filling. Squish on half the peaches and pineapple (with juice amply dripping between your fingers). Then half the raspberries and half the cream. Place second cake on top, pressing down a bit and repeat all with second half. Decorate top with toasted almonds and/or more fruit. Chill before serving.

Sweet Fruit Baked Pudding
4 servings

½   c. sugar
4   Tbs. flour
4   lg. eggs
11/3 c. milk
1   Tbs. vanilla
2   tsp. orange zest
½   tsp. almond extract
½   tsp. salt
2   c. fruit, such as sweet cherries, peaches or apricots, sliced
¼   c. brown sugar
2   Tbs. butter

Blend all but fruit, brown sugar and butter in blender till smooth.

Place cut fruit in bottom of greased 2-quart baking dish. Pour batter over all. Sprinkle with brown sugar and dot with butter.

Bake at 375° for about 40 minutes, until puffy and solid. Serve warm.

Rice Pudding-Honey Creme Brulee
8 servings

2/3 c. water
1/3 c. long grained rice
1½ c. milk
1 c. heavy cream
2 lg. whole eggs
3 lg. egg yolks
½ c. honey
2 tsp. vanilla
¼ tsp. salt
1/3 c. packed brown sugar

Simmer rice in water in small, covered pan till tender, 20 minutes. Let cool.

Heat milk and cream just to the small bubble stage.

Whip eggs, honey, vanilla, salt together well. Mix in rice. Add the hot milk in a thin stream, whisking.

Pour into buttered 9" baking dish and place in larger pan. Fill larger pan with hot water half up the sides.

Bake at 300° for 60-70 minutes, until set in middle. Cool on rack and chill in fridge 6 hours or more.

Just before serving, place in larger pan and fill sides with ice. Through sieve, spread brown sugar evenly over top of custard.

Broil 2-3 minutes close to heat, until crispy. (Don't burn!) Let cool a few minutes in ice and cut in squares. Serve with fruit garnish.

Easy Chocolate Mousse
8 servings or 1 9" pie
So easy, rich and creamy! Give the mousse 3-4 hours to chill and set.

Mix together in saucepan:
1¾ milk
½ c. sugar

Whisk together in a separate bowl:
¼ c. milk
3 egg yolks
2 Tbsp. corn starch

Bring milk and sugar to a boil, stirring a bit. Lower heat and whisk in the egg yolk mixture pouring slowly in a thin stream.

Continue to stir while mixture thickens and bubbles a bit. Take off heat and stir in till melted:
1 12 oz. package semi-sweet chocolate chips
1 tsp. vanilla

Cool completely and fold in well:
½ pint whipping cream, whipped stiff with 2 Tbsp. sugar. Place in individual bowls or prepared pie shell (see p.192). Chill several hours. Salute and serve!

Flan

6 servings

Flan is a popular Southwest dessert, but I first enjoyed it when a friend from Egypt shared it with us, many years ago. She served it as a tube pan shape, which made the delicious even more impressive.

$\frac{1}{2}$ c. sugar
2 Tbs. water

1 14 oz. can sweetened condensed milk
1 c. plus 2 Tbs. half & half
$\frac{1}{4}$ c. sugar
3 eggs
1 egg yolk
2 tsp. vanilla

Bring sugar and water to a boil in small heavy bottomed saucepan. Swirl a bit but don't stir and cook at medium heat until it changes to a deep golden brown color. Remove from heat immediately.

Pour into bottoms of 6 large custard cups and swirl up the sides a bit, working quickly.

Whisk rest of ingredients together well. Pour into custard cups.

Place in larger pan and fill around cups with 1" hot water. Bake at 325° for 40 minutes. Will be a little soft in center.

Cool and then chill in fridge 6 hours or more.

Run a sharp knife around edges and dip bottoms into hot water. Turn out on plates, scooping out remaining caramel. Serve with a bit of whipped cream or "just" plain.

Coming Up Roses

Altho encouraged many times by satisfied customers to start a restaurant, I never was too tempted, knowing the truth of the grueling work and endless hours involved, day after day. The romance of it, tho, has always allured me, and for years I went around trying to think up a good name for my kind of restaurant.

Now, I had this very nice lady customer who often had me deliver lavish amounts of party food to her absolutely charming lake-side cottage, and place it in her cute and cozy dining room up on the third floor. On impulse, one day I brought her a fancy decorative cabbage. When I handed it to her, she turned and promptly plopped it in a vase filled with a grand array of roses. A fork of lightning split the dining room air, and I found myself exclaiming, "That's it! That's the name! – "Cabbages and Roses!" And so it is. This book will have to satisfy my dreams of cafe glory. I think it truly will

"Drink to me only with thine eyes, and I will pledge with mine...."

Sweet Juice Punch
35-40 servings

Punch enough for a party!

1   1½ qt. bottle white or red grape juice
½   gal. apple juice
1   12 oz. lemonade concentrate
1   12 oz. limeade concentrate
6   c. sour cherry juice
2   liters ginger ale, chilled

Combine all ingredients except ginger ale. Chill. Add ginger ale at serving time.

For simple dressing up touches, garnish with ice cubes that have strawberries frozen in them. Or slice thinly and evenly, lemons, lime and/or oranges to float on top of punch bowl. Try floating kiwi slices or star fruit slices.

Tamarind Mango Frappe
1 serving

Tamarind, like cilantro and cumin can be found many places, like India and Mexico. It can be purchased in specialty stores and gives a distinctive tangy-sour kick to drinks. Also good as a hot, sweetened tea.

1/3   c. apple juice
1/3   c. water
3   Tbs. mango or papaya puree or chopped, fresh fruit
1   Tbs. orange juice

1   Tbs. tamarind paste
3   ice cubes

Blend all together at high speed and serve immediately.

Bedtime Ambrosia
2 servings

1   c. raw, blanched almonds
3   c. water
1   tsp. honey
♥   pinch saffron or splash rosewater

Blend almonds and water together to a frothy mush. Pour into a fine sieve over bowl and strain and press all liquid out.

Heat almond milk just until nicely warm (Too hot and it starts to make curds, which you can stir out.) Sweeten with honey and flavor with saffron and/or rosewater!

Almonds are rich in magnesium for soothing tired nerves Sweet dreams!

Indian Spiced Tea
5 servings

Here's your own homemade Chai mix

8-10 whole black peppercorns
   1 cardamom pod, shelled
   1 stick cinnamon, broken up
   2 thick slices fresh ginger, or
      1 tsp. ground ginger
   3 whole cloves
   4 c. milk
   5 tsp. black tea, good quality

Place spices in 2 qt. pot with 3 c. water. Bring to boil and boil down to half its volume. Add milk and heat till just boiling. Add tea, cover, and let steep 10 minutes. Strain and serve sweetened with honey.

Mexican Chocolate
6 servings

   4 c. milk, whole or low-fat
   ½ to 1 tsp. cinnamon or
      3" cinnamon stick
   ½ c. semi-sweet chocolate
      chips or baking chocolate,
      broken in pieces
 1/3 c. blanched, chopped
      almonds
   2 Tbs. sugar

Heat milk and cinnamon over low heat to starting-to-bubble stage: very hot and scalded.

Keep hot while blending chocolate, nuts and sugar in blender to make a coarse powder. Pour half of hot milk in blender. Cover and frappe. Add rest and whip to a froth. Serve immediately.

Garnish, if desired, with a pinch of the powder, saved out, and a splash of cinnamon.

Citrus Spritzer
10 servings

   2 c. fresh squeezed orange
      juice (5-6 oranges)
 1/3 c. fresh lime juice
   3 c. white grape juice (24 oz.)
   ❦ ice cubes
   3 c. chilled fizz water

Whip juices together and chill. Just before serving, pour 1 part sparkling water and 2 parts juice over ice cubes in glasses. Garnish with thin half slices of lime.

Cinnamon Tea

Cinnamon sticks and water, boiled 10-15 minutes. Serve sweetened with honey.

This is how it was served to me 30 years ago by Spanish friends in Santa Barbara.

Tangerine-Peach Frappe
12 servings

4 ripe peaches, peeled, sliced, or use frozen
1 Tbs. fresh lemon juice
1 6 oz. can frozen tangerine juice, or 2 c. fresh, peeled and seeded
½ tsp. cinnamon
3 c. cracked ice or ice cubes (wrapped in a towel and whacked a couple times with a hammer)

Wizz all together in blender and serve immediately with a garnish of fruit slices or fresh mint. Try others, like orange juice, mangos, guava, berries or bananas. Endless variety!

Herbal Tea Punch

Substitute strong peppermint tea for part or all of black tea in Tea Punch recipe. Unique and flavorful combination.

Fruit Lassi
4-5 glasses

2   c. plain or vanilla yogurt
1½ c. ice cubes
2   c. sweet black cherries (frozen's good)
½   c. apple juice concentrate
1   tsp. rose water
♥   large pinch cardamom

Blend all together at high speed. Serve soon as possible to maintain its chilled, frapped condition. Try substituting other fruits, such as peaches, pears, bananas, apricots, raspberries, strawberries, mango and papaya. Even cantaloupe and pineapple. Got some ripe fruit you can't use right away? Chop, freeze and use in lassi.

Tea Punch
12 servings

4   c. strong brewed aromatic tea, such as Earl Grey, spiced, or Darjeeling
4   c. apple juice
2   c. pineapple juice or orange
1   6 oz. can lemonade concentrate
☺   ginger ale or club soda

Combine all except soda. Chill. Add soda at serving time, to taste.

Index

Cabbages and Roses

Printed in the United States
56770LVS00006B/196-222

9 781595 409997